KU-714-941

teach® yourself

beginner's japanese script
helen gilhooly

For UK order enquiries: please contact Bookpoint Ltd, 130 Milton Park, Abingdon, Oxon, OX14 4SB. Telephone: +44 (0) 1235 827720. Fax: +44 (0) 1235 400454. Lines are open 09.00–17.00, Monday to Saturday, with a 24-hour message answering service. Details about our titles and how to order are available at www.teachyourself.co.uk

For USA order enquiries: please contact McGraw-Hill Customer Services, PO Box 545, Blacklick, OH 43004-0545, USA. Telephone: 1-800-722-4726. Fax: 1-614-755-5645.

For Canada order enquiries: please contact McGraw-Hill Ryerson Ltd, 300 Water St, Whitby, Ontario, L1N 9B6, Canada. Telephone: 905 430 5000. Fax: 905 430 5020.

Long renowned as the authoritative source for self-guided learning – with more than 50 million copies sold worldwide – the **teach yourself** series includes over 500 titles in the fields of languages, crafts, hobbies, business, computing and education.

British Library Cataloguing in Publication Data: a catalogue record for this title is available from the British Library.

Library of Congress Catalog Card Number: on file.

First published in UK 1999 by Hodder Education, part of Hachette Livre UK, 338 Euston Road, London, NW1 3BH.

First published in US 1999 by The McGraw-Hill Companies, Inc.

This edition published 2003.

The **teach yourself** name is a registered trade mark of Hodder Headline.

Typeset by Graphicraft Limited, Hong Kong.
Printed in Great Britain for Hodder Education, an Hachette Livre UK Company, 338 Euston Road, London NW1 3BH, by CPI Cox and Wyman, Reading, Berkshire, RG1 8EX.

The publisher has used its best endeavours to ensure that the URLs for external websites referred to in this book are correct and active at the time of going to press. However, the publisher and the author have no responsibility for the websites and can make no guarantee that a site will remain live or that the content will remain relevant, decent or appropriate.

Hachette's policy is to use papers that are natural, renewable and recyclable products and made from wood grown in sustainable forests. The logging and manufacturing processes are expected to conform to the environmental regulations of the country of origin.

Impression number   20 19 18 17 16 15 14
Year   2010 2009 2008

contents

introduction

The Japanese language presented such difficulties to 16th-century European missionaries that they called it *the Devil's tongue*. In actual fact, there are many features of the Japanese language which make it relatively straightforward to learn. The grammar, for example, follows logical rules and is very regular. It is the reading and writing of Japanese which offers the greatest challenge to the learner.

This book will make the reading and writing of Japanese accessible to you through a step-by-step approach which will help you to gradually build up your knowledge of Japanese script. The aim of this book is to show you that written Japanese can be interesting, challenging and also fun to learn.

In the Japanese education system, the learning of Japanese script is spread throughout the nine years of compulsory education. By the end of this period, the Japanese student will have learnt 1942 *kanji* (Chinese characters). This is the basic number prescribed by the Japanese Ministry of Education as essential for reading texts such as newspapers thoroughly. There are many more kanji (over 5000 in many kanji dictionaries) which are used for more specialized vocabulary and texts. Although 1942 kanji sounds like a large amount, it is worth making the comparison with English where, although we learn the alphabet relatively quickly, learning and understanding the meaning of vocabulary and different types of text takes much longer.

A brief history

The Japanese writing system was introduced into Japan by the Chinese around the middle of the 6th century AD. The Chinese language is very different to Japanese in structure and so the writing system was gradually adapted to fit the structure of the Japanese language. There are now three scripts which make up the Japanese writing system (four if you include *rōmaji* or roman script, i.e. alphabet). Let's look at each of these in turn.

Kanji 漢字

Kan is an ancient word meaning *Chinese* and *ji* means *letter* or *character*, hence kanji is translated as 'Chinese characters'. This was the script which was invented by the Chinese and introduced to Japan. Kanji are ideographs; this means that the whole character conveys a meaning or idea (whereas in the roman alphabet system, letters are grouped together to make words). For example 日 is the kanji for *sun*. Kanji were originally drawn from pictures of nature and gradually developed into the standardised kanji used today. For example 日 *sun* developed like this:

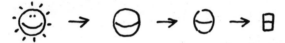

You will learn more about this in Unit 1.

There is usually more than one pronunciation for a kanji character. There are two types of pronunciation known as *onyomi* (Chinese reading) and *kunyomi* (Japanese reading). You will learn more about this in Unit 2.

Kana かな

The other two scripts in the Japanese writing system are called *hiragana* and *katakana* and are known collectively as *kana*. They are phonetic alphabets or syllabaries, which means that each symbol represents one sound only. This differs from the roman alphabet system where letters are grouped into sounds and where the same letter can be pronounced in different ways depending on its grouping (eg: **a** in rat, rate, far and fare). The difference between the Japanese phonetic system and the alphabet system can be shown through an example:

In English the word *house* is made up of five letters: *H-O-U-S-E*.

In Japanese the word for house (*uchi*) is made up of two sounds *U-CHI*. These sounds are represented by two hiragana symbols: うち

The hiragana and katakana scripts represent the same set of 46 basic sounds but the symbols are written differently and the two scripts are used for different purposes as described in the following sections.

Hiragana ひらがな

The word *hiragana* means *rounded / easy to use* and indicates both the shape and the relative simplicity of the script. Each symbol was developed from simplified kanji with the same pronunciation. For example, the hiragana symbol か (*ka*) is a simplified version of the kanji 加 (pronounced *ka*). The left side remains very similar in the hiragana symbol, the right side 'box' has been reduced to a slanting line.

Hiragana is used to write the grammatical parts of words and sentences and to write Japanese words which don't have a kanji. For example, when writing verbs (action words) the kanji is used to express the main idea or meaning and hiragana is used to indicate the function of the verb:

I listen is written: 聞きます

The kanji 聞 conveys the meaning *listen*; きます are three hiragana which show that the action is present tense *I listen*.

I listened is written: 聞きました

The same kanji 聞 conveys the meaning *listen*. The four hiragana show that it is a past action: *I listened*. You will learn more about this in Units 5 and 10.

Japanese children learn hiragana first and then gradually replace words and parts of words with kanji as they progress. Hiragana is also used to indicate how to pronounce a kanji when it is first learnt or if it is unusual. When used in this way, it is called *furigana* and is written beside or above the kanji.

Katakana カタカナ

The *kata* of *katakana* means *partial* and this is because each katakana symbol was developed from part of a kanji with the same pronunciation. For example, the katakana symbol カ (*ka*), comes from the left side of the kanji 加 (pronounced *ka*). (In this example, the same kanji is the root of both the hiragana and katakana symbol; this isn't always the case.)

The katakana script represents the same set of sounds as hiragana but the symbols are written differently and are used for different purposes. In overall appearance, hiragana symbols are rounded in shape and katakana symbols are more angular. This will become more apparent once you have worked through Units 5 and 9.

Katakana has a number of uses. Firstly, it is used for writing non-Japanese words which have been introduced into the language. These fall into two categories:

1 **Loan words** For example, ウォークマン (*wōkuman*) means *walkman*;
   テレビ (*terebi*) means *television*.

2 **Foreign names** For example, countries, cities and personal names:
   アメリカ (*amerika*) = *America*;
   パリ (*pari*) = *Paris*; スミス (*sumisu*) = *Smith*.

There are also two categories in which katakana is used for writing Japanese words:

3 **To make words stand out** Katakana makes words stand out in a similar way to writing a word in bold, italics or capitals. It is used increasingly in advertising (to make the product stand out), for slang words and exclamations, for pop group names and in headlines. Examples include: トヨタ (*Toyota*) and パチンコ (*Pachinko* – the Japanese pinball game).

4 **The classification of plants and animals**

About this book

The ten units which make up this book will gradually increase your knowledge of written Japanese. **Units 1–4** introduce mainly kanji which developed from pictures of nature. About 3% of kanji fall into this category but, as you will learn, they are also used as components of more complex kanji. **Units 4** and **6–8** will teach you how to decipher these more complex kanji giving you the tools to take your study further on completion of this book. There are plenty of hints to aid your learning and you will learn to build stories to remember the meanings of the kanji.

Units 8 and **10** give you the chance to put your learning into practice. **Unit 8** introduces you to a number of practical kanji words such as signs, notices and warnings of the kind you would see all around you in Japan. **Unit 10** introduces a number of reading passages and helps you to decipher them and extract their meaning. You will also encounter different styles of printed and handwritten text.

Two of the units are devoted to teaching the two phonetic scripts; hiragana (**Unit 5**) and katakana (**Unit 9**). There are lots of practice activities and ideas to help you learn and remember these two scripts. You can leave these units out and come back to them later if you wish to concentrate only on kanji, but if you take your study of Japanese further, then a knowledge of these scripts is essential.

There are sections throughout the book which concentrate on how to write Japanese. Again, you may wish to leave these out and concentrate on reading only.

i This symbol indicates a hint, tip or piece of information about written Japanese, to help you with your learning.

Pacing yourself

- Remember that it is YOU who sets the pace – keep enjoyment of learning at the top of your agenda!
- Find a balance between moving through the book and revising what you have learnt. Don't expect to remember everything (even Japanese people forget kanji!) and use the indexes at the back where possible to find words you have forgotten.
- Build up a set of small flashcards with kanji on one side and English on the other to test yourself from time to time. Start your own dictionary too by using a notebook or address book to write down new words.

Acknowledgements

Thank you to everyone who has advised me on the writing of this book. In particular, to Masae Sugahara and Miyuki Nagai of the School of East Asian Studies, Sheffield University – Masae for the calligraphy and for reading and commenting on the text, Miyuki for the artwork and ideas for mnemonics; to Niamh Kelly of the Japanese Department, Dublin City University for reading the text and making lots of useful suggestions; Mavis Pilbeam of the Japanese Department of the British Museum for her thorough and very helpful proofreading; Robert Gilhooly for providing the photographs; my students (including Margaret Teasdale) for being 'guinea pigs'; Sue Hart and Carolyn Taylor at Hodder and Stoughton; and John Rogers for doing all the cooking!

The publishers and author would like to thank the following for the use of material in this book: Kyoto Newspaper Company and Nobuko Kogawa (29/10/98) and Kinako Matsumoto, Seikyo Newspaper (14/9/92).

About the author

Helen Gilhooly has lived and worked in Japan, and has extensive experience of teaching Japanese and writing teaching materials at secondary school and adult level. She has an MA and a PGCE in Japanese and is the Language College Director of Aldercar Community Language College in Derbyshire. She is also a teacher trainer of Japanese at Nottingham University. Helen Gilhooly has written *Teach Yourself Beginner's Japanese* and *Teach Yourself Japanese Life, Language and Culture*.

01

第一課

unit 1

In this unit you will
- learn how Japanese script developed from pictures
- learn to read the days of the week
- begin to write

はじめに　Introduction

In the introduction to this book you learnt about the history and development of the Japanese writing system and about the three different scripts or writing forms: ひらがな (*hiragana*), カタカナ (*katakana*), and 漢字 (*kanji*). The focus of Units 1–4 is going to be on 漢字 (*kanji*) and by the end of these four units you will have learnt to recognize 58 漢字 (*kanji*) characters and also to understand the meanings of words made up from combinations of these.

漢字 (*kanji*) characters are ideographs. This means that each character represents a whole object or idea. For example:

日　is the 漢字 (*kanji*) symbol for *sun*
月　is the 漢字 (*kanji*) symbol for *moon*

As you learnt in the introduction, 漢字 (*kanji*) were written originally as pictures of the world which the ancient Chinese saw around them. These pictures were gradually, over time, standardized into regular shapes with rules about how to write them correctly. However, the pictures which each 漢字 (*kanji*) developed from can be very useful in helping you to remember the meanings. Look at these developments:

日 (*sun*) developed something like this:

As well as *sun* it also has the meaning *day*. These two concepts are connected because the rising and setting of the sun defines a day.

月 (*moon*) developed something like this:

As well as *moon* it also has the meaning *month*. These two concepts are connected because the length of a month (28 days) is measured by the progress of each new moon.

You can see from these two examples that 漢字 (*kanji*) do not necessarily have only one meaning but can represent a number of associated ideas.

Work it out!

The aim of this section is to give you the opportunity to work out for yourself the meanings of 漢字 (*kanji*) by linking them to pictures of the objects they represent. The 漢字 (*kanji*) you will start with all have meanings linked to nature and the world which surrounded the ancient Chinese. To carry out this activity, look at pictures 1–12 that follow and then see if you can link them to the 漢字 (*kanji*) a–l at the foot of this page. Try to match the shape of the pictures to the 漢字 (*kanji*) characters. がんばって (*ganbatte*) – good luck!

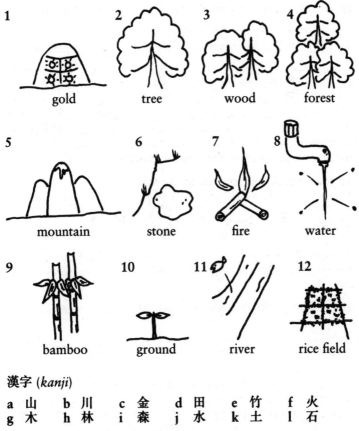

1 gold
2 tree
3 wood
4 forest
5 mountain
6 stone
7 fire
8 water
9 bamboo
10 ground
11 river
12 rice field

漢字 (*kanji*)

a 山	b 川	c 金	d 田	e 竹	f 火
g 木	h 林	i 森	j 水	k 土	l 石

Check your answers at the back of the book then look again at the pictures and see if you can envisage how the pictures became the standardized 漢字 (*kanji*) which are used today.

Explanation: Linking kanji to pictures 1

There follows an artist's impression of the progression of changes, from standardized 漢字 (*kanji*) character back to original picture.

漢字 (*kanji*) Character	絵 (*e*) Picture	英語 (*eigo*) English
山	山 → 山 → 山 → 山	mountain
川	川 → 川 → 川	river
金	金 → 金 → 金 → 金	gold/money
田	田 → 田 → 田	rice field
竹	竹 → 竹 → 竹 → 竹	bamboo
火	火 → 火 → 火	fire
木	木 → 木 → 木	tree
林	林 → 林 → 林	wood
森	森 → 森 → 森	forest
水	水 → 水 → 水 → 水	water
土	土 → 土 → 土	ground
石	石 → 石 → 石	stone
月	月 → 月 → 月 → 月	moon
日	日 → 日 → 日 → 日	sun

Did you notice how two trees are used to represent a wood and three trees a forest? You will learn more about this type of 漢字 (*kanji*) in Unit 2.

5 unit 1 第一課

練習一 Activity 1

How well can you remember the 漢字 (*kanji*) and meanings you have learnt so far? Test yourself by linking each 漢字 (*kanji*) with its English meaning. The first one is done for you.

1	山	a	water ( )
2	石	b	moon ( )
3	火	c	earth ( )
4	竹	d	river ( )
5	金	e	tree ( )
6	水	f	forest ( )
7	田	g	fire ( )
8	林	h	stone ( )
9	川	i	sun ( )
10	土	j	mountain (1)
11	木	k	rice field ( )
12	森	l	bamboo ( )
13	日	m	wood ( )
14	月	n	gold ( )

Explanation: Days of the week

Look at the 漢字 (*kanji*) that follow and remind yourself of their meanings:

日、月、火、水、木、金、土
sun, moon, fire, water, tree, gold, earth

These 漢字 (*kanji*) are also used to represent the first part of the words for the days of the week. 日 is the first part of Sunday, 月 is the first part of Monday and so forth. Here are some tips to help you remember which 漢字 (*kanji*) represents which day of the week. The first two are easy!

日 *Sun* → SUNday.

月 *Moon* → MOONday or *Monday* as it has become in English.

火 *Fire* also represents *Tuesday*. In English, Tuesday derives from the word Tiw who was the Norse god of war. If you connect the ideas of war and fire in your mind then you will remember that FIREday is Tuesday!

水 *Water* also represents *Wednesday* – easy to remember because both start with 'W'!

木 *Tree* also represents *Thursday* – both start with 'T' (but do not confuse with Tuesday).

金 *Gold/Money* also represents *Friday* – Friday is often pay day!

土 *Earth/Soil* and *Saturday*. This is the beginning of the weekend and a good day for working in the garden!

練習二　Activity 2

Link the 漢字 (*kanji*) in the left column with the corresponding day of the week in the right.

1	火	a	Monday ( )
2	日	b	Tuesday ( )
3	土	c	Wednesday ( )
4	水	d	Thursday ( )
5	月	e	Friday ( )
6	金	f	Saturday ( )
7	木	g	Sunday ( )

読む練習　Reading practice

Throughout the book, this section will give you opportunities to put into practice and further develop your reading of 漢字 you have learnt.

The 漢字 (*kanji*) in Activity 2 represent the first part of the words for the days of the week. In fact, the days of the week are written using three 漢字 (*kanji*) characters. The other two are 曜日 and they represent *day*. You already know 日 and have learnt that it can mean day. 曜 represents the concept of 'weekday' but simply remember them as together representing the day part of Monday, Tuesday, etc.

This is what the complete words for the days of the week look like in 漢字 (*kanji*):

日曜日	*Sunday*
月曜日	*Monday*
火曜日	*Tuesday*
水曜日	*Wednesday*
木曜日	*Thursday*
金曜日	*Friday*
土曜日	*Saturday*

When two or more 漢字 (*kanji*) are combined in this way to produce new words and meanings, they are called 熟語 (*jukugo*) or **compound words**. You will learn more about these in Unit 2.

By the way, you will often see the days of the week written with the first 漢字 (*kanji*) only, for example, on calendars and diary sheets. This is like writing 'Mon, Tues, Wed' in English.

練習三　Activity 3

The following is part of a music events column from a teenage magazine. Notice that the groups and events are written partly in English script. It is highly fashionable in the Japanese music world (and not only there) for group names and song titles to be written in English. The effect of the script is often far more important than the meaning of the words. (*Rancid Japan Tour* and *Michelle Gun Elephant* from the extract are just two examples of this!)

The day of the week on which each of the events will take place is written in brackets next to the date (13th–23rd). Notice that only the first 漢字 (*kanji*) for each of the days of the week is written. Now have a go at answering the questions that follow the text.

13(水)	③ROTTEN ORANGE TOUR　●場所/渋谷クラブクアトロ●料金/前売り￥3,000・当日￥3,500(1ドリンク、1CD付)●OPEN17：00・START18：00●出演/GARLIC BOYS、YELLOW MACHINGUN、ダッフルズ他。⑩SMASH WEST☎06-361-0313
15(金)	RANCID JAPAN TOUR 1999　●場所/赤坂BLITZ●料金/￥5,800●時間/OPEN17：00・START18：00●アルバム「LIFE WON'T WAIT」を引っ提げてのツアー。16、23、24日もBLITZでライブをやるぞ。⑩クリエイティブマン☎03-5466-0777
17(日)	THE MICHELLE GUN ELEPHANT 「WORLD PCHYCO BLUES TOUR "ALL STANDING／MAXIMUM.!!"」　●場所/横浜アリーナ●料金/￥4,200●時間/OPEN16：00・START18：00●アルバム「ギヤ・ブルース」が大好評のミッシェルの怒濤のスタンディングツアー。⑩ディスクガレージ☎03-5436-9600
19(火)	DOWN BEAT　●場所/西麻布YELLOW●料金/￥2,500(フライヤー持参で￥2,000・共に2ドリンク付)●時間/OPEN・START21：00●出演/DJ KEN-BO、KOYA、ATSUSHI出演のHIP HOPイベント。⑩YELLOW☎03-3479-0690
21(木)	Lauryn Hill JAPAN TOUR　●場所/日本武道館●料金/S：￥7,000・A：￥6,000●時間/START19：00●ソロアルバムが世界中で大ヒット中の彼女の待望のソロライブ。22、23日にもライブあり。⑩ウドー音楽事務所☎03-3402-5999
21(木)	ZEPPET STORE 「COMING UP ROSES TOUR'98」　●場所/渋谷CLUB QUATTRO●料金/￥3,800●時間/OPEN18：00・START19：00●シングル「ROSE」が話題のZEPPET STOREのツアー。⑩バックステージTOKYO☎03-3357-8080
22(金)	Breath 「3ヶ月無料ライブ」　●場所/恵比寿ギルティ●料金/無料●時間/OPEN18：30・START19：00●ハードなライブが魅力のバンド、Breathが現在3ヶ月無料ライブを実施中。入場方法などは、インフォメーション☎03-5467-2544まで問い合わせてみてね。
23(土)	WORLD CONNECTION "KOOL"　●場所/西麻布YELLOW●料金/￥3,000（フライヤー持参で￥2,500・共に2ドリンク付)●時間/OPEN・START21：00●出演/DJ：KO KIMURA、FUJIMOTO VJ：E-MAIL⑩YELLOW☎03-3479-0690

On which day of the week do the following events take place?

1 Rotten Orange Tour
2 Down Beat
3 The Michelle Gun Elephant . . . Tour
4 Rancid Japan Tour
5 World Connection 'Kool'.

How many events are taking place on:

6 a Friday
7 a Saturday
8 a Thursday?
9 Which day of the week is not represented in the events extract?

書く練習一 Writing practice 1

This section will introduce you to some simple rules for writing 漢字 (*kanji*). You will learn some further rules in Unit 2 and will then practise writing some of the 漢字 (*kanji*) you have learnt.

The rules for writing 漢字 (*kanji*) are very precise and Japanese children spend many hours of their school life learning and practising the correct order for writing each 漢字 (*kanji*). (In a similar way, we learn how to write the letters of the alphabet correctly at school.) Each single part of a 漢字 (*kanji*) is called a stroke and the order in which 漢字 (*kanji*) are written is called 書き順 (*kakijun*) or *stroke order*.

The Japanese use squared paper when they are learning how to write because it helps to ensure that 漢字 (*kanji*) are all the same size and are balanced correctly. If you can, use large squared graph paper which is subdivided into four smaller squares during the initial stages of learning to write. This will help you to balance left and right, and top and bottom of each 漢字 (*kanji*). Alternatively you could use ordinary graph paper and have four smaller squares making up one larger square. The 漢字 (*kanji*) taught in the earlier units will also have an example written in this type of square so that you can copy exactly from the book. Once you feel confident, you can use clear squares or use smaller squared paper / graph paper for practising and perfecting your technique.

Here are some simple rules to get you started and examples to copy.

Rule 1: **Horizontal** 漢字 (*kanji*) strokes are written from left to right.

例 (*rei*) Example: *three*

Rule 2: **Vertical** 漢字 (*kanji*) strokes are written from top to bottom.

例 (*rei*) Example: *river*

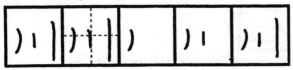

Rule 3: Where the 漢字 (*kanji*) character has an intersecting horizontal and vertical stroke, the starting stroke is usually the horizontal one (but there are some exceptions).

例 (*rei*) Example: *earth*

Notice you work downwards; the final stroke is the bottom horizontal one.

Rule 4: A left-hand diagonal line is written before a right-hand diagonal line.

例 (*rei*) Example: *tree*

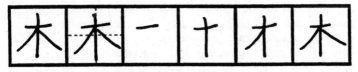

Rule 5: Here is a square 漢字 (*kanji*).

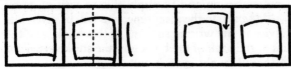

Rule 6: When the square contains other strokes within it, you fill in this part before writing the bottom line of the square.

例 (*rei*) Example: *sun*

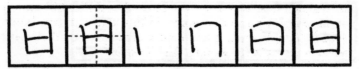

You can combine these rules you have learnt to write 石 (*stone*):

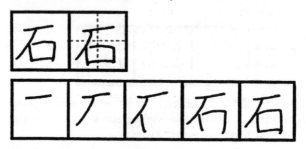

Using these six rules, you have learnt to write the following 漢字 (*kanji*) in this section:

三、川、土、木、日、石
(*three, river, earth, tree, sun, stone*)

Now see if you can write them on squared paper in the correct order from memory (refer back to the rules to check when you have finished).

As a final note in this section, although it is important to understand and apply the basic rules for writing 漢字 (*kanji*), there are some aspects of stroke order which do not fall easily into rules and so you also need to learn and practise the stroke order for each 漢字 (*kanji*) character. Do not be daunted by this, however, because 'practice makes perfect' and if you write 漢字 (*kanji*) over and over again and concentrate on the correct stroke order you will begin to develop a feel for the order in which they are written. You will also begin to develop your own way of remembering and to apply this to writing more complicated 漢字 (*kanji*). In the meantime, you will be given lots of help and advice in the writing sections of this book, and the unit summaries at the back of the book give the stroke order for the main 漢字 (*kanji*) taught in each unit.

終りに Conclusion

This section in each unit will summarize the main aspects of the unit. In addition, Units 2, 4, 6 and 8 contain a test so that you can evaluate how well you have remembered the 漢字 (*kanji*) you have learnt up to that point. In this unit you have learnt 14 漢字 (*kanji*), seven compound words (days of the week) and six basic rules for writing 漢字 (*kanji*).

The following terms and sub-headings have been used in this unit:

第一課	*dai ikka*	unit 1
はじめに	*hajime ni*	introduction
漢字	*kanji*	kanji (Chinese characters)
練習	*renshū*	activity/practice
読む練習	*yomu renshū*	reading practice
書く練習	*kaku renshū*	writing practice
例	*rei*	example
終りに	*owari ni*	conclusion

Other key words and terms are given in the conclusion of Unit 2. Refer to these if you want to say the terms and sub-headings used throughout this book in Japanese.

02

第二課

unit 2

In this unit you will
- add some new 漢字 (*kanji*) to the 14 you have learnt already
- learn the Japanese pronunciation of these 漢字 (*kanji*)
- apply your learning to real reading situations
- learn more about writing Japanese script

はじめに　Introduction

1　Can you remember the meanings of the 漢字 you were introduced to in Unit 1? You can see them in the following list, so test yourself and check back to Unit 1 if there are any you are unsure about.

山　川　日　月　土　竹　森　木　水　田　金　林　火　石

2　Can you remember which 漢字 represents which day of the week? They are listed below in their full form. Remember it is the first 漢字 which tells you which day of the week it is.

月曜日　日曜日　土曜日　木曜日　火曜日　水曜日　金曜日

Again, check back to Unit 1 if you are unsure of any them.

Work it out!

In this section, as with Unit 1, you will be introduced to some new 漢字 through the pictures of natural objects that they are derived from. Most of the 漢字 introduced in this unit are associated with the human body. Try matching the pictures (1–12) with the 漢字 (a–l) on the following page (without looking at the answers!). In two cases (*eye* and *car/vehicle*) you may need to imagine the pictures turned on their side to identify them.

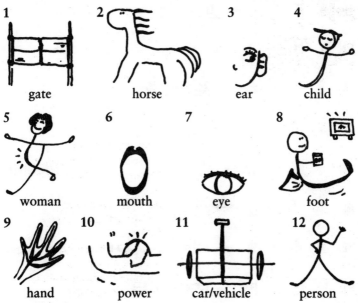

1　gate

2　horse

3　ear

4　child

5　woman

6　mouth

7　eye

8　foot

9　hand

10　power

11　car/vehicle

12　person

a 口　　b 足　　c 目　　d 女　　e 子　　f 人
g 耳　　h 手　　i 力　　j 車　　k 馬　　l 門

Explanation: Linking kanji to pictures 2

An artist's impression of the changes from standardized 漢字 back to picture follows. Check your answers to the previous activity with this sequence.

漢字	絵 (e) Picture	英語 (eigo) English
人	人 人 → 犬 → 犬 → 犬	person
女	女 女 → 女 → 女 → 女	woman
子	子 子 → 子 → 子 → 子	child
目	目 目 → 目 → 目 → 目	eye
耳	耳 耳 → 月 → 月 → 月	ear
口	口 口 → ○ → ○ → ○	mouth
手	手 手 → 手 → 手 → 手	hand
足	足 足 → 足 → 足	foot
力	力 力 → 力 → 力 → 力	power/strength
馬	馬 馬 → 馬 → 馬 → 馬	horse
車	車 車 → 車 → 車 → 車	cart/vehicle/car
門	門 門 → 門 → 門 → 門	gate

In this set of new 漢字 there is an example of an abstract noun, 力 (*power/strength*), being portrayed in picture form through the image of the muscles in the arm. Another point of interest is that 車 originally developed from the picture of a cart which would have been the type of transport or vehicle used when 漢字 were first developed. In modern times it has taken on the meaning of *car*.

Kanji build up

This section in this unit and throughout the book will introduce you to new 漢字 and new words based on the 漢字 you have learnt so far.

1 Complex kanji

The pictorial 漢字 that you have been introduced to so far not only have meanings in themselves but are also used as parts or components of 漢字 that are more complex. You actually learnt two of these more complex 漢字 in Unit 1. They were 林 (*wood*) and 森 (*forest*). Both are created from 木 (*tree*) – two trees represent a wood, three trees a forest. Here are four more 漢字 built from simpler ones which you have learnt already. The meanings of the components are incorporated into these complex 漢字 forms. Notice that the simpler 漢字 when used as components of more complex 漢字 may change their shape slightly or appear 'squashed'.

男 (*man*) – This is made from the components 田 (*rice field*) and 力 (*power*). In other words, the **man** uses his **power** to work in the **rice fields**.

好 (*like, love*) – This is a combination of 女 (*woman*) and 子 (*child*). The abstract idea of love is expressed through the **love** between **women** and **children**.

明 (*bright*) – This is a combination of 日 (*sun*) and 月 (*moon*). The **sun** and **moon** shining together would create a very **bright** light.

本 (*root, origin*). 木 (*tree*) with a horizontal line through the **trunk** indicates the root of the tree.

Unit 4 will look at these complex 漢字 in more detail but you can see from these examples that a knowledge of the simpler 漢字 can also help you to decipher the more complex ones.

2 Kanji compounds

The four 漢字 you have just been introduced to are created by combining simpler 漢字 to form one complex 漢字. Another way in which 漢字 are used to create new meanings is by forming words from two or more separate 漢字. You have already been introduced to this idea through the days of the week. Three separate 漢字 are used to make up each day. For example, 月曜日 means Monday. Here are some more examples:

人口 means *population* ('people's mouths' = number of mouths to feed)
馬力 means *horse power*
女子 means *girl* ('woman child')
(Notice that these are two separate 漢字, unlike 好 (complex 漢字) which means love/like.)
日本 means *Japan* ('sun's root' describes Japan as the place east of China where the sun rises. This is where the term 'land of the rising sun' comes from).

To summarize the two points in this section: 漢字 can join together and form one 漢字 (for example, 男) or they can form words made up of two or more 漢字 (for example, 人口).

練習一 Activity 1

Some compound words made up of two or three 漢字 follow. Can you work out their meanings? (You may want to look back at the 漢字 you have learnt so far in Units 1 and 2 and refresh your memory before trying this activity.)

| a 水力 | b 男子 | c 日本人 | d 馬車 | e 人力 |
| f 人力車 | g 水田 | h 火山 | i 門口 | j 人目 |

Once you have thought about the possible meanings of these words, look at the list of English words that follows and decide which best fits each 漢字 before you check the answers at the back of the book.

1 volcano   2 boy   3 Japanese person
4 carriage   5 in the public eye   6 water power
7 gateway   8 manpower
9 a rickshaw (man-pulled carriage)
10 a paddy field (a field flooded with water for wet rice growing)

Explanation: Working out the meaning

You will have noticed that sometimes the meanings are a direct 'translation' of the separate 漢字 into their new meaning. For example, 火山 ('fire mountain' or *volcano*). In other cases you need to think more laterally or abstractly. For example, 人目 (*in the public eye*). However, once you know what the meanings are they are easy to remember because the pictorial 漢字 act as a visual jog to the memory. And words are created in a very logical fashion. For example, 人力車 means literally 'human-powered vehicle' and that is what a rickshaw is as the following illustration shows.

In fact, the word *rickshaw* is a corruption of the Japanese word *jin-riki-sha*. *Jin* (*person*) has been dropped and the other two words (*power*, *vehicle*) have had their pronunciation 'anglicized'. Try saying the Japanese *rikisha* and you'll see what I mean!

復習　Review

Before continuing any further, here is an activity to help you review the single 漢字 learnt so far in this unit.

Match the following 漢字 with their English meanings from the selection in the box. Then try the activity in reverse by taking the English meanings from the box first.

人、力、車、耳、女、明、口、子、男、好、手、目、馬、門、本、足

vehicle	man	eye	root	person	bright
ear	foot	woman	gate	hand	child
mouth	like	horse	power		

If there are any of these characters that you are not sure about, look back through the unit and check your answers.

読む練習 Reading practice

The way in which dates are written in Japanese is interesting. You were introduced to the 漢字 for *moon* 月 and *sun* 日 in Unit 1 and you also learnt that these 漢字 have the connected meanings of *day* 日 and *month* 月 – so let us look at how this works in practice. This is how a typical Japanese calendar looks for the month of January:

1月[a]						
日	月	火	水	木	金	土[b]
1日	2日	3日	4日	5日	6日	7日[c]
8日	9日	10日	11日	12日	13日	14日
15日	16日	17日	18日	19日	20日	21日
22日	23日	24日	25日	26日	27日	28日
29日	30日	31日				

a is the month written in numerals and 漢字. Japanese months do not have a name as such, so they are assigned a number from 1 to 12. Therefore, **6月** is *June* (the sixth month), **1月** is *January* (the first month) and **12月** is *December*.

b are the 漢字 for the days of the week (as you learnt in Unit 1). They are shortened in this case to just the first 漢字 of the three which you learnt (for example, 水曜日 means *Wednesday*) because this is all that is needed to identify each day of the week. (This is rather like writing *Tues*, *Wed*, etc. in English.)

c are the days of the month. Each number is followed by 日 (similarly in English we follow the dates with *st*, *nd*, *rd* or *th*. For example, 1*st*, 7*th*).

練習二 Activity 2

Using the calendar and information just given, try answering the following questions.

1 On which day of the week is **a** 1st **b** 4th **c** 9th **d** 14th?
2 How many days in the month fall on a Wednesday and what are they?
3 On which day of the week will **1月1日** fall?

(Note that Japanese dates are written in the order: month then date.)

練習三　Activity 3

At the foot of this page is a calendar from a Japanese travel brochure. Look at it and answer questions 1–4.

1 What are the starting and finishing months on this calendar?
2 In which months do the following happen:

   a the 2nd is a Tuesday
   b the 24th is a Monday
   c the 6th is a Friday?

3 On what day of the week is:

   a May 5th
   b October 26th
   c February 18th
   d August 21st
   e December 25th?

4 On what days of the week do these Japanese festivals fall:

   a Girls' Day (March 3rd)
   b New Year's Day
   c Tanabata (Star Festival, July 7th)
   d Golden Week (April 29th–May 5th)
   e Emperor's Birthday (December 23rd)?

4月

日	月	火	水	木	金	土
	1	2	3	4	5	6
7	8	9	10	11	12	13
14	15	16	17	18	19	20
21	22	23	24	25	26	27
28	29	30				

5月

日	月	火	水	木	金	土
			1	2	3	4
5	6	7	8	9	10	11
12	13	14	15	16	17	18
19	20	21	22	23	24	25
26	27	28	29	30	31	

6月

日	月	火	水	木	金	土
						1
2	3	4	5	6	7	8
9	10	11	12	13	14	15
16	17	18	19	20	21	22
23/30	24	25	26	27	28	29

7月

日	月	火	水	木	金	土
	1	2	3	4	5	6
7	8	9	10	11	12	13
14	15	16	17	18	19	20
21	22	23	24	25	26	27
28	29	30	31			

8月

日	月	火	水	木	金	土
				1	2	3
4	5	6	7	8	9	10
11	12	13	14	15	16	17
18	19	20	21	22	23	24
25	26	27	28	29	30	31

9月

日	月	火	水	木	金	土
1	2	3	4	5	6	7
8	9	10	11	12	13	14
15	16	17	18	19	20	21
22	23	24	25	26	27	28
29	30					

10月

日	月	火	水	木	金	土
		1	2	3	4	5
6	7	8	9	10	11	12
13	14	15	16	17	18	19
20	21	22	23	24	25	26
27	28	29	30	31		

11月

日	月	火	水	木	金	土
					1	2
3	4	5	6	7	8	9
10	11	12	13	14	15	16
17	18	19	20	21	22	23
24	25	26	27	28	29	30

12月

日	月	火	水	木	金	土
1	2	3	4	5	6	7
8	9	10	11	12	13	14
15	16	17	18	19	20	21
22	23	24	25	26	27	28
29	30	31				

1月

日	月	火	水	木	金	土
			1	2	3	4
5	6	7	8	9	10	11
12	13	14	15	16	17	18
19	20	21	22	23	24	25
26	27	28	29	30	31	

2月

日	月	火	水	木	金	土
						1
2	3	4	5	6	7	8
9	10	11	12	13	14	15
16	17	18	19	20	21	22
23	24	25	26	27	28	

3月

日	月	火	水	木	金	土
						1
2	3	4	5	6	7	8
9	10	11	12	13	14	15
16	17	18	19	20	21	22
23/30	24/31	25	26	27	28	29

練習四　Activity 4

Convert the following random dates into English as in the examples. Remember the Japanese order: **month, date, day.**

例 *Rei* 1　8月3日（火）= Tuesday August 3rd (order: August 3rd Tuesday)

例 *Rei* 2　10月26日（金）= Friday October 26th

a　2月14日（土）　　b　11月20日（木）　　c　5月5日（月）
d　9月10日（日）　　e　12月25日（水）　　f　4月1日（金）

漢字の読み方　Kanji readings

This section will teach you about reading 漢字 in Japanese. As suggested in the Introduction, if you wish to focus on just understanding the meaning of 漢字 then you can miss these sections out throughout the book or come back to them later.

1　*Kunyomi* (訓読み) and *onyomi* (音読み)

In the Introduction you learnt that there are two ways of reading 漢字 in Japanese, the *kunyomi* (訓読み) or Japanese reading and the *onyomi* (音読み) or Chinese reading. The *onyomi* has developed from the original Chinese pronunciation but over the centuries it has been adapted to and become part of the Japanese language. The *kunyomi* is the native Japanese word.

For example, 川 (*river*) can be pronounced *SEN* (*onyomi*) and *kawa* (*kunyomi*). *Kawa* was the Japanese word for 'river' and so when 漢字 were introduced from China this word was linked to the 漢字 character 川.

By the way, notice that *kawa* (*kunyomi*) when written in *rōmaji* (romanized script or alphabet) is written in lower case and *SEN* (*onyomi*) in upper case. This system is used in many 漢字 workbooks and dictionaries and is also followed in this book.

2　Rules for using *kunyomi* and *onyomi*

As a general rule, the *kunyomi* is used for single 漢字 words whereas the *onyomi* is used for compound 漢字 words of two or more 漢字. Here is an illustration of this.

a Single 漢字 words

人 (*person*) is pronounced *hito* (*kunyomi*)
口 (*mouth*) is pronounced *kuchi* (*kunyomi*)

b Compound 漢字 words

The above 漢字 make up the compound word 人口 (*population*) which is pronounced *JINKŌ*.
JIN and *KŌ* are the *onyomi* of 人 and 口 respectively.

There will be further examples and the opportunity to practise new information and rules as you progress through the book so do not worry if you have understood only some of the details so far. There are exceptions to the rules about when to use *kunyomi* and *onyomi* but these will be pointed out to you when necessary and explained, and there will be lots of reinforcement activities too.

練習五 Activity 5

In this unit you are going to concentrate on the *kunyomi* (Japanese reading) only. In the following list are the 漢字 you learnt in Unit 1 with their *kunyomi* and a guide to how to pronounce these readings. Look over these and practise saying them. Then see how well you can remember them by covering up the *kunyomi* column, looking at the 漢字 and saying them from memory.

漢字	Meaning	*Kunyomi*	Pronunciation
山	mountain	*yama*	ya-ma (*a* of *mat*)
川	river	*kawa*	ka-wa (*a* of *mat*)
金	gold/money	*kane*	ka-ne (*a* of *mat*, *e* of *end*)
田	rice field	*ta*	ta (*a* of *mat*)
竹	bamboo	*take*	ta-ke (*a* of *mat*, *e* of *end*)
火	fire	*hi*	(*i* of *hit*)
木	tree	*ki*	(*i* of *hit*)
林	wood	*hayashi*	ha-ya-shi (*a* of *mat*, *i* of *hit*)
森	forest	*mori*	mo-ri (*o* of *hot*, *i* of *hit*)
水	water	*mizu*	mi-zu (*i* of *hit*, *u* of *blue*)
土	ground, earth	*tsuchi*	tsu-chi (*tsu* is one syllable, *chi* of *chin*)
石	stone	*ishi*	i-shi (*i* of *hit*)
月	moon	*tsuki*	tsu-ki (*tsu* is one syllable, *i* of *hit*)
日	sun	*hi*	(*i* of *hit*)

ℹ️ Pronunciation rules

There are five vowel sounds in Japanese. These are *a*, *i*, *u*, *e* and *o*. They are always pronounced in the same way. A general guide to their pronunciation can be seen in the list just given and can be summarized as follows:

- *a* as in *mat*
- *e* as in *end*
- *i* as in *hit*
- *o* as in *hot*
- *u* as in *blue*

These vowels are attached to consonants to make new sounds but remember, the pronunciation of each vowel remains constant. The sound *tsu* is an unfamiliar one in English – it is one beat or syllable, 'squash' the *t* and *s* together as you say it.

You may have noticed that the readings of 火 (*fire*) and 日 (*day*) are the same – they are both pronounced *hi*. There are many examples of Japanese words which have the same pronunciation but are written with different 漢字. The difference in meaning can be understood from reading the 漢字 or from the context. There are many examples in English, too, of words which are pronounced in the same way but which have different meanings. These differences in meaning are indicated by the spelling or the context or both.

練習六　Activity 6

How well can you remember the *kunyomi* reading and pronunciation of each 漢字? You may want to look back at the readings on the previous list and practise saying them out aloud – looking at the 漢字 as you do so – before trying the following activity.

i　Tick the correct 漢字:

		a		**b**		**c**	
1	*ta*	a	竹	b	田	c	川
2	*mori*	a	土	b	林	c	森
3	*ishi*	a	金	b	石	c	土
4	*kawa*	a	川	b	山	c	水
5	*ki*	a	日	b	火	c	木

ii　This time tick the correct *kunyomi*:

		a		**b**		**c**	
1	金	a	*kane*	b	*kawa*	c	*ki*
2	竹	a	*ta*	b	*hayashi*	c	*take*
3	月	a	*tsuchi*	b	*tsuki*	c	*ishi*
4	林	a	*hayashi*	b	*ki*	c	*mori*
5	水	a	*mori*	b	*kawa*	c	*mizu*

iii Now you are going to test your understanding of the three aspects of 漢字 you have learnt – the 漢字 itself, the *kunyomi* and the meaning in English. You will link these three aspects by choosing one from each of two categories (a–c and i–iii) to match the first item as in the examples:

例	*Rei* 1	*ta*	a	月		b	日		c	田√
			i	rice field√		ii	moon		iii	gold

例	*Rei* 2	月	a	*tsuki*√		b	*tsuchi*		c	*hi*
			i	day		ii	moon√		iii	earth

1	fire	a	水	b	木	c	火
		i	*ki*	ii	*hi*	iii	*mizu*

2	森	a	*mori*	b	*hayashi*	c	*ishi*
		i	wood	ii	tree	iii	forest

3	*yama*	a	川	b	竹	c	山
		i	mountain	ii	river	iii	wood

4	gold	a	木	b	金	c	火
		i	*kawa*	ii	*kane*	iii	*mori*

5	竹	a	wood	b	bamboo	c	river
		i	*take*	ii	*tsuki*	iii	*tsuchi*

6	*mizu*	a	water	b	moon	c	forest
		i	火	ii	木	iii	水

7	stone	a	田	b	石	c	日
		i	*ishi*	ii	*tsuchi*	iii	*ki*

8	土	a	sun	b	moon	c	earth
		i	*tsuchi*	ii	*tsuki*	iii	*ishi*

9	*kawa*	a	川	b	水	c	竹
		i	bamboo	ii	gold	iii	river

10	林	a	wood	b	forest	c	tree
		i	*mori*	ii	*hayashi*	iii	*ki*

練習七 Activity 7

The following activity gives you the opportunity to use the *kunyomi* for 漢字 learnt so far in a real reading situation. Japanese surnames are made up of either single 漢字 or two or three compounded together. The 漢字 used in surnames are often fairly simple ones including some of those you have learnt in Units 1 and 2. Although 漢字 used in surnames have literal meanings (for example, the surname 竹山 (Takeyama) literally means 'bamboo mountain'), the Japanese do not think of them in this way. Many English surnames also have literal meanings (for example, Rivers, Hill, Robinson) but again, they are known as names not meanings.

When saying Japanese surnames you use the *kunyomi*. You learnt at the beginning of this section that in general the *onyomi* is used for compound 漢字 words. However, names are an exception to this rule.

Can you say these common surnames in Japanese:

a 林	b 森田	c 森山	d 山川
e 竹山	f 森	g 木田	h 石川

For the following surnames (i–m), 田 is pronounced *da* instead of *ta*. How do you say these names?

i 金田　　j 竹田　　k 石田　　l 山田　　m 川田

書く練習二　Writing practice 2

In Unit 1 you learnt some basic rules for writing 漢字. Now you are going to revise these rules with some new 漢字 you have learnt in this unit. You will also learn some further rules and, once you are familiar with these, you will have a go at writing 漢字 in the correct order.

Rules 1–3: You learnt in Unit 1 that you write from left to right and from top to bottom. Usually, where two lines intersect, the highest horizontal line is written before the vertical line, and then you work downwards. For example, *hand*. Note: the short top stroke is written from right to left.

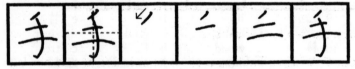

Rule 4: Diagonal lines follow the same rule of writing the left diagonal before the right. For example, *person*.

Rule 5: You also learnt in Unit 1 how to write a square. This is how *mouth* is written (notice that the shape is different from the square).

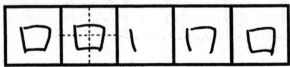

Rule 6: When there is a middle part to the square, you write the bottom line last. For example, *eye*.

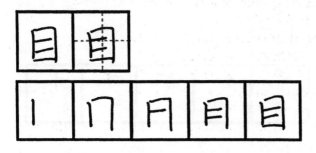

And *rice field* (but notice this is an exception to Rule 3 because the vertical intersecting line inside the square is written before the horizontal).

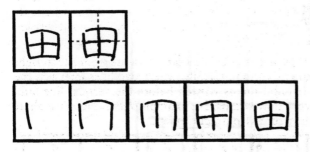

Here are two further rules.

Rule 7: Where a 漢字 has a distinct left and right part, the left section is written before the right and where it has a distinct top and bottom part, the top section is written first. For example, *wood*.

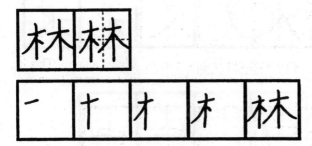

Note that the left section is narrower than the right.

And *forest* is similar.

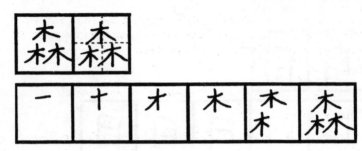

You combine Rules 5, 6 and 7 to write *gate*.

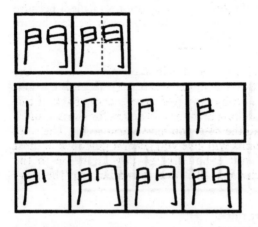

Rule 8: Where a 漢字 is symmetrical with a central 'axis', you write the 'axis' first followed by the left side and then the right side. For example, *water*.

And *mountain* is another similar instance.

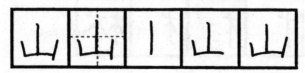

練習八　Activity 8

Can you write the following 漢字 applying the rules you have been introduced to so far? Remember to use squared paper to achieve the right balance and proportions.

Rules 1–4:

川 (*river*)　　三 (*three*)　　力 (*power*)　　人 (*person*)

Rules 5 and 6:

日 (*sun*)　　月 (*moon*)　　田 (*rice field* – exception to Rule 3)

Rule 7:

林 (*wood*)　　竹 (*bamboo*)

Rule 8:

小 (*small* – Unit 6)　　水 (*water*)　　山 (*mountain*)

You can check your answers by looking back through the writing sections of Units 1 and 2. For 力, 月, 竹 look up their stroke order in the unit-by-unit 漢字 charts at the back of this book. Then use the writing sections and charts for Units 1 and 2 to practise writing all the 漢字 you have learnt so far. The rules given in these two units will give you general guidance in most cases but they are not exhaustive so pay attention to the stroke order for individual 漢字 and remember that there are exceptions to rules.

終りに　Conclusion

In this unit you have been introduced to 16 new single 漢字 as well as 14 compound 漢字 words and 13 Japanese surnames. You have also learnt to read dates and have been introduced to the readings of some 漢字. And you have reviewed writing rules and learnt two new ones.

The following new terms and sub-headings have been used in this unit:

復習	*fukushū*	review
漢字の読み方	*kanji no yomikata*	kanji readings
訓読み	*kunyomi*	Japanese reading
音読み	*onyomi*	Chinese reading
テスト	*tesuto*	test

テスト　Test

This section is designed to test how well you have remembered what you have learnt in Units 1 and 2.

1 The 漢字 below are grouped by theme. Which is the odd one out?

   a Parts of the body: 目、足、男、手、耳

   b Days of the week: 月、土、火、水、日、林

   c People and animals: 馬、子、力、男、女

   d Abstract ideas: 好、金、明、力

2 What do these compound 漢字 words mean? (**f** is a new word):

   a 人口　　**b** 日本　　**c** 女子

   d 門口　　**e** 火山　　**f** 男女

3 Match these dates to the festivals and holidays on the right:

   a 12月25日　　　i April Fool's Day

   b 1月1日　　　　ii Christmas Day

   c 7月4日　　　　iii Hallowe'en (October 31st)

   d 3月21日　　　iv May Day (May 1st)

   e 4月1日　　　　v Spring Equinox (March 21st)

   f 10月31日　　　vi New Year's Day

   g 5月1日　　　　vii American Independence Day (July 4th)

4 Can you say these Japanese surnames? (* indicates a change in pronunciation from *ta* to *da*):

   a 山田*　　**b** 竹山　　**c** 森田　　**d** 森　　**e** 石田*

5 Can you write the following 漢字 in the correct stroke order?

土、日、目、手、木、水、山、田

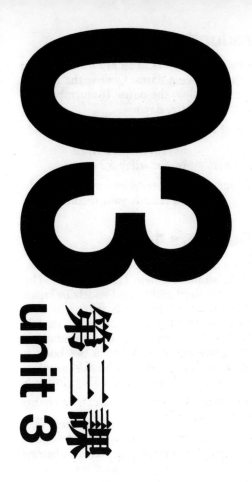

03

unit 3　第三課

In this unit you will
- learn to read numbers in Japanese
- use these numbers in real reading situations
- practise writing 漢字

はじめに　Introduction

In Unit 2 you learnt how to read dates. You are now going to review this by reading the following dates. Choose the English equivalent from the selection below the dates. (Remember that the order in Japanese is month, date, day.)

a　4月21日（火）　　**b**　11月5日（土）　　**c**　9月10日（水）

i　Wednesday 21 April　　iii　Tuesday 21 April
ii　Wednesday 10 September　iv　Saturday 5 November

If you are still unsure about reading dates then look back at the section on dates in Unit 2 (p. 18) to refresh your memory.

Explanation: Numbers 1–10

Two systems of numbering have already been used in this book. One of these is the arabic number system (1, 2, 3 . . .). This system is internationally recognized and is used widely in Japan. However, every language has its own words when counting (English: *one, two, three* . . . ; French: *un, deux, trois* . . . etc.). In Japanese there are 漢字 which represent the words for numbers. They have been used alongside arabic numbers in this book to number activities and explanations. These are the 漢字 numbers 1–10:

一、二、三、四、五、六、七、八、九、十

The following section gives some tips for memorizing these 漢字 and you may already have thought of some. First, though, a word on how they developed. These 漢字 represent abstract concepts and so instead of developing from pictures, they are made up of a series of points and lines. You have learnt one other abstract 漢字 so far – 力 (*power/strength*). This looks similar to the 漢字 for *nine* 九 so look carefully at the difference. There is also a picture to help you remember the difference: you bend your arm inwards to flex your muscle (力); 九 has a Q-shape. Now look at the pictures.

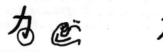

ℹ️ Remembering the numbers 1

Here are some tips for remembering the 漢字 for numbers:

一、二、三 (*1*, *2*, *3*) are easy as you have probably noticed – 'one line, two lines, three lines'

四 is a four-sided square and so is easy to relate to the number *4*.

五 When you look at this 漢字, you can trace the arabic number *5* in it. Try it!

六 The number *6* in Japanese is pronounced *roku* – not unlike the English word *rocket*! With a little imagination, you should see a rocket taking off in this 漢字!

七 If you turn this 漢字 upside down, a continental number *7* emerges.

七 ⁷ × ¹ ↱ → 七

八 The arabic number *8* turned on its side is also the mathematical symbol for infinity. Imagine that the 漢字 is a road leading into the distance and on into infinity!

九 With a lot of imagination this looks like a combination of the 漢字 for 8 and for 1, and of course 8 + 1 = *9*.

十 The roman numeral for *10* is X. This looks like the 漢字 tilted to one side.

You may find your own ways of remembering these and other 漢字. I find that it really helps to try to associate a new 漢字 with an idea or picture in your mind (and you will be learning more about this in future units). Once you have begun to remember new 漢字 you will probably not need to refer to these ideas again but they can really help at first.

練習一　Activity 1

1 Match the sequence of 漢字 numbers on the left with their equivalent sequences on the right:

a　一、二、三、四　　　　i　3, 6, 9
b　十、九、八、七　　　　ii　2, 4, 6, 8
c　一、三、五、七　　　　iii　8, 9, 10
d　三、六、九　　　　　　iv　1, 2, 3, 4
e　二、四、六、八　　　　v　1, 3, 5, 7
f　八、九、十　　　　　　vi　10, 9, 8, 7

2 The following sequence of numbers 1–10 is out of order. Point at each of these 漢字 numbers in sequence then look back to p. 30 to check that you are correct:

三、五、六、一、九、八、二、十、四、七

3 The odd one out. The following sequences of 漢字 numbers all have one number missing when matched with the arabic numbers on the right. Which number is it?

a　一、二、三、四、五　　　1, 2, 3, 4, 5, 6
b　十、八、六、二　　　　　10, 8, 6, 4, 2
c　四、六、七、八　　　　　4, 5, 6, 7, 8
d　二、四、六、十　　　　　2, 4, 6, 8, 10

Kanji build up: Numbers 11–99

These are easy to read because they are logically made from combinations of the 漢字 numbers 1–10. It is not necessary to write them all out for you, but here are the numbers 11–21 (in sequence) to give you an idea of how it works.

十一、十二、十三、十四、十五、十六、十七、十八、十九、二十、二十一

Can you see the pattern? The numbers 11–19 are made up of 10 plus the relevant unit:

十一 = 10 + 1 = 11;　十二 = 10 + 2 = 12

20 is made up of a 2 in front of a 10: 二十. Remember the order like this: $2 \times 10 (= 20)$. You then add the relevant unit to make 21, 22, 23, and so on:

二十一 = $2 \times 10 + 1$ = 21
二十二 = $2 \times 10 + 2$ = 22
二十三 = $2 \times 10 + 3$ = 23

練習二　Activity 2

1 The numbers 20, 30, 40, 50, 60, 70, 80, 90 follow in sequence. Look at them and make sure you can recognize them before moving on to the next activity.

二十、三十、四十、五十、六十、七十、八十、九十

2 Now the same sequence has been jumbled up. Return the numbers to the original sequence by pointing at each in turn. Then check with the above sequence to see if you are right.

六十、九十、二十、四十、七十、五十、三十、八十

3 How are you getting on so far? Remember you can always look back to earlier sections if you need to refresh your memory. Next you are going to practise reading the sequence of numbers from 21–30. This time they have already been jumbled up. Can you put them in the correct sequence?

a 二十九	**b** 二十三	**c** 二十六	**d** 二十七
e 二十四	**f** 二十八	**g** 二十二	**h** 二十一
i 二十五	**j** 三十		

Now check your answers at the back of the book.

4 Finally, in this section you are going to pull together everything you have learnt so far about numbers and have a go at reading a random selection of numbers between 1 and 99! Try writing down your answers in arabic numbers and then checking them at the back of the book. がんばって (*ganbatte*) – good luck!

a 九	**b** 六	**c** 七	**d** 十九
e 十七	**f** 十三	**g** 二十	**h** 五十
i 七十	**j** 二十一	**k** 三十二	**l** 四十三
m 五十四	**n** 六十五	**o** 七十六	**p** 八十七
q 八十八	**r** 九十九		

How did you get on? You might find that this is a good place to take a break and digest what you have learnt so far before moving on to the next section.

Kanji build up: Five new kanji

百 100　千 1000　万 10,000　円 yen (Japanese currency)
年 year

Here are some visual clues and ideas to help you associate each
漢字 with its meaning:

百 (100)　　Turned on its side the 漢字 looks like this:
　　　　　　ᗒᗕ → ᗒᗕᗕ You can trace the numerals 100
　　　　　　in this.

千 (1000)　This looks like the 漢字 for ten (十) but with an
　　　　　　extra part on the top in the same way that 1000
　　　　　　looks like 10 but with 2 extra zeros!

万 (10,000)　In the Western counting system we count in
　　　　　　thousands until we reach one million. The
　　　　　　Japanese system of counting is slightly different.
　　　　　　Instead of saying ten thousand, there is an extra
　　　　　　word to represent this amount. Hence the 漢字
　　　　　　symbol 万. If you look carefully at this, you can
　　　　　　see a leaning 'T' on the left and, ignoring the line
　　　　　　at the top, you can also make out the shape of an
　　　　　　'h'. Using a little twisted logic (!) you can let the T
　　　　　　represent 'ten' and the Th represent 'thousand' –
　　　　　　ten thousand!

To work out larger amounts of this unit, multiply the number by
10,000. For example:

十万 = 10 × 10,000 = 100,000
百万 = 100 × 10,000 = 1,000,000

円 The Japanese currency is the yen, represented by this 漢字
and by the international symbol ¥. All currencies can be written
in words or numerals. For example: *six pounds* or £6, *six dollars*
or $6, and in Japanese:

Words: 六円　　Numerals: ¥6

The character 円, because it is a suffix to money amounts, is easy
to recognize and remember.

年 Here is a visual image for remembering this 漢字:

Can you make out the left half of the 漢字 for bamboo (竹) at the front and a house shape behind? In Japan, bamboo decorations are put outside the front of houses at New Year, hence the visual clue leads you to the meaning *year*.

Look back over this section and remind yourself of the visual clues to the meanings; then try the next section.

練習三　Activity 3

1 Put these multiples of 100 into the correct order (100–900). Which one is missing?

a 九百	b 三百	c 五百	d 四百
e 百	f 二百	g 八百	h 七百

2 How do you write these 漢字 number amounts in arabic numbers?

a 八千	b 五千	c 七千	d 六千
e 二千	f 千 (or 一千)		

3 Match these multiples of 10,000 with their arabic number equivalent below them:

　a 二万　　b 九万　　c 九十万　　d 百万　　e 千万

i 90,000	ii 1000,000	iii 20,000
iv 900,000	v 10,000,000	

4 Combinations of 百、千、万

Put these amounts in order from the smallest to the largest:

a 二百	b 二千二百	c 二百万	d 二十万
e 二千	f 二千万	g 二万	

Now write out these amounts (in the new order) in arabic numbers.

5 Match the 漢字 money amounts on the left with their equivalent on the right:

a 三百円	i ¥7500
b 五千円	ii ¥300
c 百五十円	iii ¥3000
d 四百五十円	iv ¥70,000
e 七万円	v ¥5000
f 七千五百円	vi ¥450
g 三千円	vii ¥150

Explanation: More about dates

There are a number of ways in which the year can be written in Japanese. Let us look at these using the year 1999 as the model. Notice that the 漢字 for year (年) is written after the numbers.

1 千九百九十九年   This is 1999 written out in full using 漢字 numbers

2 一九九九年   Here 1999 is written as it looks, 1–9–9–9

3 1999年 ⎫
   99年 ⎬ The year is written in arabic numbers, notice that 年 is still used.

The first example is rarely used and the most commonly used is the third. Zero is usually written as **0**.

練習四　Activity 4

1 In this activity you are going to match the years written in 漢字 with those in arabic numerals:

1	一九六三年	a	2000 年
2	一八六三年	b	1963 年
3	二000年	c	1960 年
4	一六一六年	d	1616 年
5	一九六0年	e	1863 年

2 Now match the dates written in 漢字 with those written in arabic:

1	十一月十一日	a	6月24日
2	六月十八日	b	3月31日
3	十月二日	c	6月18日
4	八月二十一日	d	11月11日
5	三月三十一日	e	8月21日
6	六月二十四日	f	10月2日

Dates are most often written with arabic numerals but not always.

3 Now write out the dates 1–6 above in English.

Explanation: The Japanese calendar

Used alongside the Western calendar in Japan is the Japanese system of 年号 (*nengō*) or 'era names'. An era is defined by the length of rule of each Emperor. The present Emperor, Akihito, began his reign (the Emperor in modern Japan has a symbolic role with no political power) in 1989 and the new era is called

平成 (Heisei) which means 'Attainment of Peace'. The previous era was called 昭和 (Shōwa) which means 'Enlightened Peace'. Once an Emperor has died, he is referred to by the name of his era. Akihito's father, Hirohito, who died in 1989 is, therefore, now referred to as Emperor Shōwa. The 昭和 (Shōwa) era lasted for 63 years from 1926–89.

When the year is written according to the 年号 (nengō) system, it follows this pattern:

平成十一年　Heisei 11th year

To match this to the Western calendar, you count up from and including 1989 which was Heisei 1st Year. Therefore:

平成十一年 = 1999

Arabic numbers can also be used: 平成11年

昭和 (Shōwa) years are counted from and including 1926. A good way of calculating these is to have an 'anchor' year, for example, your year of birth, then count from here:

昭和三十八年　(Shōwa 38th year) = 1963

Alternatively, add 25 years to the Shōwa year to get the Western year, or take 25 years away from the Western year to arrive at the Shōwa year:

昭和二十年　(Shōwa 20th year) = 20 + 25 = (19)45
1985 = 85 – 25 = 昭和六十年　(Shōwa 60th year)

練習五　Activity 5

1　Match the following 平成 (Heisei) years with their Western calendar equivalents:

a　平成四年　　i 1994
b　平成十年　　ii 1990
c　平成七年　　iii 1997
d　平成六年　　iv 1992
e　平成九年　　v 1998
f　平成二年　　vi 1995

The first year of an era is written not with 一 (one) but with 元 which means *beginning*:

平成元年 = Heisei 1st year (1989)

2　Match the following 昭和 (Shōwa) years with their Western calendar equivalents. Remember to add 25 years to the Shōwa year:

a	昭和四十八年	i	1939
b	昭和二十五年	ii	1926
c	昭和六十三年	iii	1973
d	昭和十四年	iv	1988
e	昭和四十三年	v	1950
f	昭和元年	vi	1968

読む練習 Reading practice

This section will pull together everything you have learnt in this unit and give you the opportunity to read numbers and dates in authentic contexts.

練習六 Activity 6

1 漢字 numbers are most often used when the text is written vertically (see Question 3, p. 39). Japanese business cards are often produced with the Japanese script written vertically on one side and the romanized script (for the benefit of non-Japanese clients) written horizontally on the other. The following phone numbers are written horizontally. Notice that the area code is in brackets and a horizontal line (~) separates the two parts of the phone number. Do not confuse this with the number 一 (*one*). Can you convert them into arabic numerals?

a (0三)　三五八　～一三七七
b (0九七)　五九二　～四二一一
c (0七二0)　二一　～三八六六
d (0三)　三五九三～二七0四
e (0二七九)　二二一　～三一五四

2 The following is part of a newspaper advertisement for a series of three conferences. When will the conference be held (give the full date) in:

a London (ロンドン)
b Tokyo (東京)
c Dusseldorf (デュッセルドルフ)?

ロンドン '98年 12月 5日(土)

東京 '98年 12月 6日(日)

デュッセルドルフ '98年 12月12日(土)

3 The advertisement reproduced here is for a Japanese theatre production. Give the year, month, date and day of the performance in the Western calendar.

平成七年十月二十一日土

漢字の読み方　Kanji readings

In this section you are going to focus on saying the numbers 1–10 in Japanese. If you have worked through *Teach Yourself Beginner's Japanese*, this is in Unit 2. Otherwise, turn to the 漢字 chart for Unit 3 (pp. 190–1) and learn to say the *onyomi* reading for the numbers 1–10. Turn back to the section in Unit 2 (p. 22) if you need to re-check the pronunciation rules.

ℹ Remembering the numbers 2

Try memorizing how to say the numbers in Japanese by relating them to English-sounding words. For example, 一 (*ichi*) and 二 (*ni*) sound like 'itchy knee'!

練習七　Activity 7

Align the numbers that follow with their 漢字 and *onyomi* reading. Check your answers against the Unit 3 漢字 chart at the back of the book.

漢字	英語 (*eigo*) English	音読み (*onyomi*)
三	one	SHICHI
五	two	KYŪ
六	three	NI
一	four	SHI
八	five	ICHI
九	six	HACHI
二	seven	JŪ
十	eight	ROKU
四	nine	GO
七	ten	SAN

書く練習三　Writing practice 3

In Units 1 and 2 you learnt eight basic rules for writing 漢字 and you practised writing all the 漢字 you had learnt in those units. Next you are going to learn three simple rules for improving the shape of your strokes by looking at stroke endings. The Japanese learn calligraphy in order to perfect the shape of 漢字 using brushes but if you pay attention to these three rules, you will be able to improve the way in which you write 漢字 even with a pen or pencil. The three main types of stroke ending are as follows:

1　STOP ending.
　Your pen/pencil stops
　and lifts off the page.

2　GRADUAL STOP.
　You pull the pen gradually
　off the page with a
　sweeping motion.

3　FLICK.
　The stroke flicks up at
　the end.

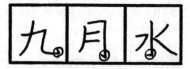

Now you are going to try writing the numbers 1–10 on squared paper (do not look at the stroke order that follows yet). Employ the eight rules you have learnt, the only exception is the number

9 where the vertical (left-hand) line is written first. Think about the stroke endings too from the previous examples.

How did you get on? The numbers 1–10 follow, written out for you. Look at the stroke order and the shapes and proportions of the strokes (for example, the left side of eight is a different shape to the right side, and the same for four and six; the strokes of two and three are not all the same length) then try to copy them as closely as possible.

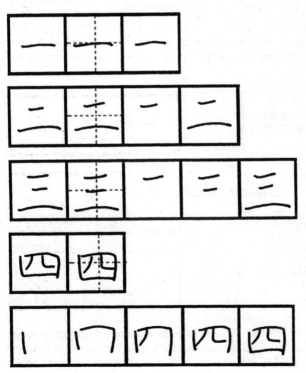

終りに　Conclusion

In this unit you have been introduced to numbers up to 10,000 through 13 漢字. You have also learnt the 漢字 for *yen* and for *year*. You have put this learning into practice to read number and money amounts, dates and telephone numbers. You have also learnt about the Japanese calendar and have been introduced to two compound 漢字 words for the present and previous eras. Altogether, you have learnt 15 single 漢字 (plus related compounds) and three new compound words (平成、昭和、年号). You have learnt to count in Japanese from 1–10 and have applied the writing rules you learnt previously to writing 漢字 numbers.

04

第四課
unit 4

In this unit you will
- learn to recognize 12 漢字
  used in action words (verbs)
- be introduced to words
  made up of combinations
  of these and other 漢字
- learn more about
  pronouncing and
  writing 漢字

はじめに　Introduction

In Unit 2 you learnt that some 漢字, as well as having meanings in themselves, are used as components of more complex 漢字 (see p. 15). The 漢字 you will be introduced to in this lesson are created from simpler 漢字, some of which you have learnt already. In the following activity you are going to review some key 漢字 to refresh your memory before moving on to learning the new 漢字 in this unit.

1 Can you remember the meanings of the 漢字 that follow?

　　a 口　　b 耳　　c 人　　d 目　　e 山
　　f 門　　g 木　　h 日　　i 子

2 Now look at the new 漢字 in the following list. They each contain simple 漢字 as part of their structure. Can you spot them? (You do not need to know the meaning of the whole 漢字 at this stage.)

　　a 聞　　b 見　　c 書　　d 言
　　e 学　　f 買　　g 休　　h 出

Check the answers to these two activities in the back before moving on to the next section.

Explanation: Finding clues

The new 漢字 introduced in the second activity you have just completed can all be used as verbs (that is, action or doing words). So far, you have not learnt the meaning of any of them but you have identified simpler 漢字 within them. These can be a clue to their meanings and you are going to use these clues to work out the meanings for yourself. Before you can do this, here are three extra pieces of information.

1 This shape 儿　(　) when used as a 漢字 component has the meaning 'human legs'. You can see it in 2b of the introduction above.

2 This shape 八　(　) has the meaning 'animal legs'. You can see it in 2f.

3 The 漢字 for person (人) takes this form 亻 when used as part of a more complex 漢字. You can see an example of this in 2g.

練習一　Activity 1

The following seven 漢字 (a–g) all represent verbs. The story clues (1–7) link the different components of each 漢字 into a story which indicates the 漢字 meaning. (The component meanings are in **bold**.) This technique should help you to remember that meaning. Now can you work out which 漢字 has which meaning?

a 聞　　b 見　　c 言　　d 学　　e 買　　f 休　　g 出

Story clues

1　A **person** resting by a **tree** during their work break. *Meaning: to rest; holiday.*
2　An **eye** running around on **human legs**. *Meaning: to look, watch or see.*
3　**Mountains** upon **mountains** but somewhere there is a way out. *Meaning: to go out.*
4　A neighbour is pressing an **ear** between the **gates** of the house to hear the gossip. *Meaning: to hear or listen.*
5　An **eye** with **animal legs** is a shellfish. A sideways **eye** above it is a human inspecting it before buying. *Meaning: to buy.*
6　At school the **child** is expected to wear a special **hat** when studying. *Meaning: to study.*
7　The **mouth** spoke words which rose up in **lines**. *Meaning: to say; words.*

How did you get on? There follows the same 漢字 this time with their meanings and a picture representation as well:

ear at the gates.
聞 to listen, to hear

Let's go to see!
=3　見 to see, watch, look

言 to say
blah blah …

学 to study

z z z
休 to rest

I'll have this, please.
買 to buy

Way Out
出 to go out

Now read through the stories again. Do you see how the components of these 漢字 help to indicate their meanings?

練習二　Activity 2

This is a quick activity designed to help you review the 漢字 learnt so far in this unit. Simply match the 漢字 on the left with the meanings on the right.

1 買　　　　　a　to listen
2 休　　　　　b　to look
3 出　　　　　c　to say
4 聞　　　　　d　to study
5 学　　　　　e　to go out
6 見　　　　　f　to buy
7 言　　　　　g　to rest

練習三　Activity 3

Here are seven more 漢字 which you are going to learn in this lesson:

売　読　話　書　食　飲　入

Some of the components which make up these 漢字 are contained in the following list. Can you locate and ring the appropriate part on the 漢字 above? The number in brackets indicates the number of times the component appears.

1 儿 human legs (× 2)
2 言 to say (× 2)
3 口 mouth (× 3)
4 土 earth (× 2)
5 日 sun (× 1)
6 千 1000 (× 1)

How did you get on? You can find the answers in the explanations that follow.

Explanation: More kanji components

The handwritten 漢字 which follow have had their component parts numbered. These numbers are referred to in the explanations. A story is given to help you remember the meaning.

1 This upper part looks like 土 (*earth*) except that the top horizontal line is longer, like this: 士. In fact this 漢字 means *samurai* but when used as part of a more complex 漢字 we are going to take its meaning as *earth*.
2 In between the legs and the earth is a table.
3 'Human legs'.

Story: **People walked** over to the **tabletop** sale to see a **samurai** selling clods of **earth**.
Meaning: *to sell* 売.

1 You should have identified *to say / words* (言) at the left of this 漢字.
2 Can you see that this is the same as the 漢字 you have just learnt (*to sell*: 売)?

Story: Notice outside a bookstore: '**Words for sale.** Buy a book and read the **words**'.
Meaning: *to read* 読.

1 Once again, the left side is *to say / words*.
2 1000 (千).
3 *mouth* (口). Together 2 and 3 make up the 漢字 for *tongue* (舌).

Story: **Thousands of words** were spoken by the **tongue**.
Meaning: *to talk, speak* 話.

1 This comes from a 漢字 you have not learnt yet, *brush* (筆). Before pens were invented, writing was done with calligraphy brushes. Here is a picture to help you link the meaning to the character:

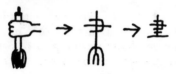

2 You will have recognized this as *sun*. An alternative meaning is *mouth* (口) with a line in it (日). You could think of this as a condensed version of 言 (*to say*) with the words about to come out of the mouth.

Story: Written **words** are created by a **calligraphy brush**.
Meaning: *to write* 書.

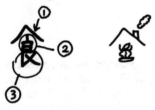

1 Think of this as a roof, in this case, the roof of a house.
2 This means *white* and represents the sun with a ray coming off it. In ancient China the rays of the sun were seen as white.
3 This lower part is actually a truncated version of 火 (*fire*) which you learnt in Unit 1.

Story: **White** rice boiled over a **fire** in a Japanese **home**.
Meaning: *to eat*; *food* 食.

1 You have just been introduced to the left side of this 漢字. It is slightly truncated but indicates the same meaning, *food*.
2 A more detailed picture of the right side will help you with the meaning.

Story: The left side gives the general meaning (**food**). The right side is a person taking a **drink**.
Meaning: *to drink*; *a drink* 飲.

Notice the difference between the handwritten and printed versions (入) of this 漢字. And do not confuse it with *person* (printed = 人; handwritten = **人**).

In this new 漢字 the 'person' appears to be walking back across the page. The printed version shows this 'person' clearly indicating their direction (flick at the top points to the left).

Story: **People** going in walk to the **left**.
Meaning: *enter, go in* 入.

練習四　Activity 4

This is a review activity for you to test yourself on the second set of 漢字 you have just learnt. Match the 漢字 on the left with the meanings on the right.

1	食	a	drink
2	入	b	eat
3	売	c	read
4	書	d	talk
5	飲	e	enter
6	話	f	sell
7	読	g	write

How did you get on? If you are still uncertain about some of these, read through the stories and look at the composition of each 漢字 again, until you are sure.

読む練習　Reading practice

You now know the first 漢字 of the instruction in this heading – it means *read*. Before you try this next section, let us summarize the 漢字 you have learnt in this unit. First look at the 漢字 and see if you can remember the meaning before looking at the English beneath them.

1 聞	2 見	3 書	4 言	5 学
6 買	7 休	8 出	9 売	10 読
11 話	12 食	13 飲	14 入	

1 listen	2 look	3 write	4 say	5 study
6 buy	7 rest	8 go out	9 sell	10 read
11 speak	12 eat	13 drink	14 enter	

練習五　Activity 5

Here are some sentences in Japanese followed by some in English overleaf. At this stage you will not be able to read the whole sentence because you have not learnt *hiragana* yet (Unit 5). There is also one 漢字 (語)* which you have not seen yet. However, you will be able to understand the key words of the sentence from your knowledge of 漢字. By matching these with the full English sentences you will be able to get the meaning of the whole sentence. For example:

男の人は車を買いました。　*The man (male person) bought*
2　2　　2　4　　　　　*a car.*

The 漢字 you have already learnt have numbers below them. These refer to the unit in which the 漢字 was first introduced so that you can check back if you need to. Did you notice that the verb comes at the end of the sentence? The order would sound like this: *the man a car bought*. In the sentences this will appear in brackets (marked as *lit.*). Now have a go yourself. がんばって! *ganbatte*! Good luck!

1　女　人は　　日本語*を　学びました。
　　2　2　　　1 2 (7)　　4
2　女の子は　土曜日に　休みました。
　　2 2　　　1　　　　4
3　男の人は　月を　見ました。
　　2 2　　1　　4
4　林さんは　森田さんに　話しました。
　　2　　　1 2　　　　　4
5　男の子は　馬が　好きです。
　　2 2　　2　　2
6　女の人は　竹の子を　食べました。
　　2 2　　1　2　　4
7　山田さんは　車を　売りました。
　　2 1　　　2　　4

Match each one to its Japanese partner in the list on p. 50 (not in order).

a The woman (female person) ate some bamboo shoots (bamboo children). (*lit.* The woman some bamboo shoots ate.)

b The girl (female child) rested on Saturday. (*lit.* The girl on Saturday rested.)

c Mr Yamada (Mountain-rice field) sold his car. (*lit.* Mr Yamada his car sold.)

d The boy (male child) likes horses. (*lit.* The boy horses likes.)

e The woman (female person) studied Japanese. (*lit.* The woman Japanese studied.)

f Mr Hayashi (Wood) talked to Mrs Morita (Forest-rice field). (*lit.* Mr Hayashi to Mrs Morita talked.)

g The man (male person) looked at the moon. (*lit.* The man at the moon looked.)

How did you get on? Check your answers at the back of the book.

Kanji build up: More kanji compounds

In this section you will be introduced to some new compound 漢字 words. First you need to learn a new 漢字:

物 *thing*

This 漢字 is used to make verbs into nouns. This is best explained with an example:

買 (*to buy*) + 物 (*thing*) = 買物 = *shopping* (*lit.* buying things)

練習六 Activity 6

The 漢字 compounds that follow have been made into nouns by adding 物 (*thing*) to them. Can you work out what their meanings would be in English? There is a list of English words in random order beneath the 漢字 words which you can refer to if you need to.

1 飲物　**2** 食物　**3** 売物　**4** 見物　**5** 書物　**6** 読物

a writing　　　**b** food　　　**c** items for sale
d sightseeing　**e** book　　　**f** drinks

練習七　Activity 7

Here are some more compound words using 漢字 you have been introduced to in this unit. See if you can work out their meanings by matching them with their English equivalents on the right.

1	売買	**a**	a study visit
2	読書	**b**	start school
3	入学	**c**	eating and drinking
4	出入	**d**	absence from school (long term)
5	飲食	**e**	reading
6	見学	**f**	buying and selling
7	休学	**g**	going in and out

練習八　Activity 8

This activity introduces compound 漢字 words which use 漢字 from the first four units of this book. Think about the literal meaning and then see if you can work out what you would say in English. The box of English words (in random order) will act as a checklist once you think you have worked out the meaning of a word. Here are some amusing examples to get you started!

例 *Rei* 1　出目金　*lit.* go out eye gold = *a pop-eyed goldfish*
例 *Rei* 2　休火山　*lit.* resting fire mountain = *a dormant volcano*
例 *Rei* 3　二足　*lit.* two feet = *two pairs (of footwear)*

1	売人	2	入口	3	出口	4	飲水
5	学力	6	買手	7	休日	8	日本人

buyer	dealer (seller)	entrance	Japanese person
exit	drinking water	holiday	academic ability

漢字の読み方　Kanji readings

You were first introduced to how 漢字 are pronounced in Unit 2 and you can refer back to that unit for guidance on pronunciation (p. 22). In this section in Unit 3 you used the kanji chart at the back of the book to learn the *onyomi* (Chinese readings) of the numbers 1–10. Now turn to the chart for Unit 4 on pages 191–2 which contains all the single 漢字 introduced in this unit. Focus on the *onyomi* readings and try to memorize them. Here are some hints to help you.

ℹ️ Memorizing kanji readings

1 Look back at the simple pronunciation rules you were given in Unit 2 (p. 22).

2 Say the readings out loud.

3 See if you can match each reading to an English word and make a little story to help you remember. For example, the *onyomi* of 食 (*eat*) is *SHOKU*. So how about: 'It was a *SHOCK* how much food he could eat!' And the *onyomi* of 見 (*look*) is *KEN* so: '*KEN* looked out of the window.' Do you get the idea?

4 Test yourself by covering up the reading, looking at the 漢字 and saying the reading out loud.

Now try Activity 9.

練習九　Activity 9

1 This is a simple linking activity. Link the 漢字 on the left with their correct reading:

1	買	a	*DOKU*
2	休	b	*SHOKU*
3	出	c	*NYŪ*
4	聞	d	*BAI* (use twice)
5	学	e	*KYŪ*
6	見	f	*SHUTSU*
7	言	g	*WA*
8	食	h	*BUN*
9	入	i	*KEN*
10	売	j	*IN*
11	飲	k	*GAKU*
12	話	l	*SHO*
13	書	m	*GEN*
14	読		

2 Now try saying these compound 漢字 words in Japanese:

a 売買 (buying and selling)
b 読書 (reading)
c 入学 (start school)
d 出入 (going in and out)
e 飲食 (eating and drinking)
f 見学 (study visit)
g 休学 (absence from school)
h 見聞 (knowledge; experience)

書く練習四　Writing practice 4

You should now recognize the first 漢字 in this heading – it means *write*. In this section you are going to learn to write the 14 漢字 which have been introduced in this unit. Remember: stroke order is important for writing accurately, for helping you to remember the 漢字 and for counting the number of strokes. And there are sometimes slight differences between handwritten and printed versions of the same 漢字.

ℹ Writing kanji

One way to remember how to write more complex 漢字 is to visualize the components they are made up of. For example, in preparing yourself to write 聞 (*listen*) from memory, say to yourself 'gate and ear'. Look carefully at the proportions and overall balance of each 漢字. For example, where a 漢字 has a distinct left and right side, the left side is narrower (the proportions are approximately left side = 1/3; right side = 2/3).

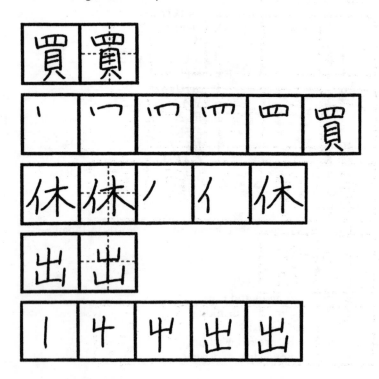

聞	聞

門	門	門	門

聞	聞	聞

学	学

丶	丷	丷	丷

丷	学	学	学

見	見	目	貝	見

言	言

丶	亠	三	言	言

食	食

ノ	八	人	今	今

今	食	食	食

入	入	ノ	入

売	売

一	十	士	吉	吉	声	売

飲	飲

ノ	人	人	今	今	會

食	食	食	飲	飲	飲

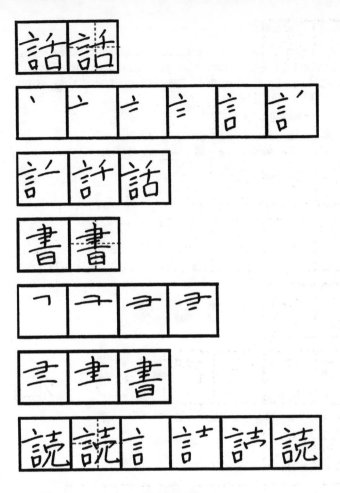

終りに Conclusion

In this unit you have been introduced to 14 漢字 which represent action words and have learnt to pronounce their *onyomi* and to write them. You have also learnt the meanings of 26 compound 漢字 words and have identified the key words in a set of Japanese sentences. Now try the test to see how well you have remembered the 漢字 you have learnt in the first four units!

テスト Test

The 漢字 (including some compound words) you have learnt so far are grouped in themes. Can you remember their English meanings? (Some 漢字 appear more than once if they cover more than one category.)

1 People and animals

   a 馬   b 人   c 女   d 男
   e 子   f 女子   g 男子   h 日本人

2 Elements of nature

   a 山   b 火山   c 川   d 水   e 火
   f 木   g 林   h 森   i 田

3 Numbers and money

   a 一   b 五   c 六十円   d 百
   e 四千円 f 二万   g 金   h 三千七百

4 Dates

   a 九月十一日 (土)   b 八月二十日
   c 一九九一年   d 平成十二年

5 Verbs (action words)

   a 聞   b 食   c 飲   d 言   e 話
   f 読   g 売   h 見   i 買   j 休

6 Parts of the body

   a 耳   b 口   c 足   d 目   e 手

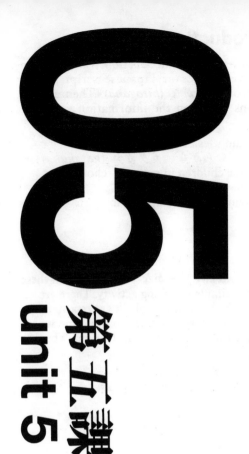

05

第五課

unit 5

In this unit you will
- learn to read the 46 ひらがな (*hiragana*) symbols which make up the phonetic 'alphabet'
- learn some rules for making extra sounds from the 46 main symbols
- be introduced to picture–sound associations to make learning easier
- learn how to write ひらがな (*hiragana*)
- have a go at reading some words and phrases

はじめに　Introduction

Look back to pages viii–x of the Introduction which give an overview of the different types of Japanese script and in particular the section on ひらがな (*hiragana*). Then answer the following questions based on the information you have just read.

1　What are the two main uses of ひらがな?
2　Which script (漢字、ひらがな、カタカナ (*katakana*)) is learnt first by Japanese children in primary schools?
3　What did ひらがな develop from?
4　How many basic symbols make up the modern ひらがな syllabary?

Work it out!

You have not learnt to read any ひらがな yet (apart from these four symbols) but try this simple matching activity. There are six ひらがな words (a–f) in the left column which are repeated in a different order in the right column. Match up the same words and write the correct letter in the brackets on the right. The first one is done for you.

a	すし	つくえ	( )
b	あき	せいと	( )
c	こえ	すし	(a)
d	つくえ	こえ	( )
e	きとう	あき	( )
f	せいと	きとう	( )

Explanation: How to read hiragana

Let us begin by looking at the first four lines of the ひらがな syllabary with the romanized pronunciation and learn how to read them.

Notice that the chart is written in the traditional way, from top to bottom and from right to left. Therefore, you read in columns rather than rows. And you begin to read from the top right-hand corner. Can you now answer these two questions:

ta た	*sa* さ	*ka* か	*a* あ
chi ち	*shi* し	*ki* き	*i* い
tsu つ	*su* す	*ku* く	*u* う
te て	*se* せ	*ke* け	*e* え
to と	*so* そ	*ko* こ	*o* お

1 What is the first ひらがな symbol?
2 Which column do you read first and in what order?

To save you looking in the back, the answers are 1 あ *a*
2 あ *a*、い *i*、う *u*、え *e*、お *o*.

The next point to notice is that the first five sounds are what we call vowel sounds. In Unit 2 (p. 22) you were introduced to the pronunciation of Japanese sounds. A quick checklist follows to help you remember the pronunciation.

あ	*a*	as in *mat*	え	*e*	as in *end*
い	*i*	as in *hit*	お	*o*	as in *hot*
う	*u*	as in *blue*			

And, as you also learnt in Unit 2, consonants are attached to each of these vowels to create new sounds. Each of these sounds is represented by a ひらがな symbol. This is why the Japanese syllabary is called 'a phonetic alphabet'. (The roman alphabet consists of 26 letters which are used in various combinations to create a range of sounds.)

練習一 Activity 1

In the 'Work it out!' activity on p. 60 you matched six ひらがな words. This time you are going to try to read these words. Use the chart of the first 20 symbols on p. 62 and see if you can say the words. Their English meanings are written in brackets.

a すし (sushi) **b** あき (autumn)
c こえ (voice) **d** つくえ (desk)
e さとう (sugar) **f** せいと (school pupil)

Explanation: The hiragana chart

You are now going to be introduced to the whole ひらがな chart (pp. 62 and 63), including the correct order to write each symbol. To help you understand the layout of the chart, an explanation is now given using the first symbol あ.

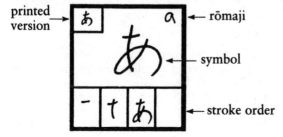

na	ta	sa	ka	a
な	た	さ	か	あ
に (ni)	ち (chi)	し (shi)	き (ki)	い (i)
ぬ (nu)	つ (tsu)	す (su)	く (ku)	う (u)
ね (ne)	て (te)	せ (se)	け (ke)	え (e)
の (no)	と (to)	そ (so)	こ (ko)	お (o)

The printed version of each symbol is also included (top left-hand corner) because this sometimes differs slightly from the handwritten version.

Have a go at writing the ひらがな because this will help you to remember how to read them. The basic rules you learnt for 漢字 also apply here – you write horizontal strokes from left to right, and vertical/diagonal strokes from top to bottom. As you write each one (using graph paper if possible), say its sound to yourself.

練習二　Activity 2

The activities in this unit will keep referring you back to the different charts, so do not worry about learning all the symbols at once! There is also a section later to help you explore ways to remember the 46 basic ひらがな symbols but first here is an activity to get you reading.

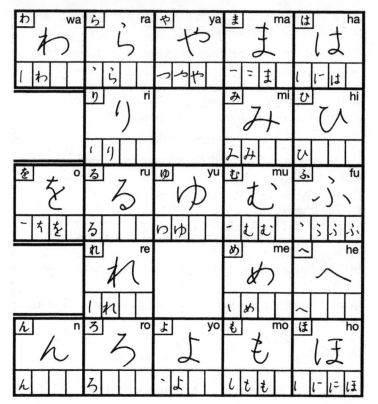

Each sequence of ひらがな symbols in the activity is taken from a column, row or diagonal of the chart. Try to read (out loud) each of the ひらがな, then refer back to the relevant part of the chart to refresh your memory. Then try again to read the sequence from memory. Continue like this until you can read the sequence confidently, then move on to the next one.

The first part of this activity refers to the first page of the chart (p. 62).

1 The third column (always count from the right): さ、し、す、せ、そ
2 The third row (reading from right to left): う、く、す、つ、ぬ
3 The diagonal from top left to bottom right: な、ち、す、け、お
4 The diagonal from top right to bottom left: あ、き、す、て、の
5 The second column: か、き、く、け、こ
6 The fourth row: え、け、せ、て、ね

Have you noticed that the syllables in the row sequences always end with the same vowel sound?

Now look at the sequences 1–6 again and answer these questions:

7 How many times do the symbols **a** し **b** き **c** て appear?
8 Which symbol appears three times?
9 Which symbol appears the most times?

(Answers to 7–9 are at the back of the book.)

The second part of this activity refers to the second page of the chart (p. 63).

10 The first column: は、ひ、ふ、へ、ほ
11 The fourth column: ら、り、る、れ、ろ
12 The fifth row: ほ、も、よ、ろ、ん
13 The diagonal from top left to bottom right: わ、り、ゆ、め、ほ
14 The diagonal from top right to bottom left: は、み、ゆ、れ、ん

Now look at the sequences 10–14 again and answer these questions:

15 How often do the symbols **a** れ and **b** ん appear?
16 How many symbols only appear once?
17 Which symbol appears the most times?

(Answers to 15–17 are at the back of the book.)

ℹ Remembering hiragana

This section will introduce you to a way of remembering ひらがな through visual and sound association (mnemonics). The basic idea is that you find a way to make the shape of each symbol suggest a picture or story which connects it to its sound. For example, here are some ideas for the first five ひらがな. Concentrate on the sounds (for example, *aim* = e) rather than the letters or spellings.

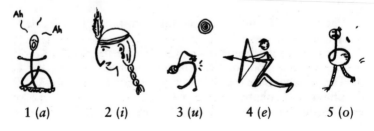

1 (*a*) 2 (*i*) 3 (*u*) 4 (*e*) 5 (*o*)

Stories

1 あ (*a*) is an opera singer singing an _aria_ (Japanese pronunciation has a short 'a' sound)
2 い (*i*) is an American _Indian_ 4 え (*e*) _aim_ for the target
3 う (*u*) _ooh_, my back hurts! 5 お (*o*) is an _ostrich_

Do you get the idea? Here are another ten to get you started, then, if you find this method helps you, try to think of your own. You might not have inspiration for all of them at first, but try a few at a time and write down your ideas in a notebook.

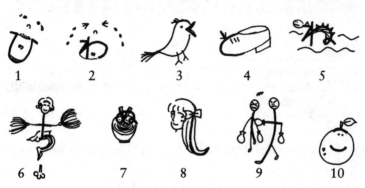

Stories

1 ひ (*hi*) is someone laughing, _hee_ hee
2 わ (*wa*) is a baby crying, _waaaa_
3 く (*ku*) for _cuck_oo
4 と (*to*) is the _toe_ of a shoe
5 ね (*ne*) is the Loch _Ness_ monster
6 ち (*chi*) is a _cheer_leader
7 ぬ (*nu*) looks like a bowl of _noo_dles
8 し (*shi*) _she_'s got long hair
9 け (*ke*) for _KO_ (knocked out)
10 こ (*ko*) is a _Cox_ apple

練習三　Activity 3

Now that you have been introduced to the 46 ひらがな symbols, it is time to put your learning into practice and try reading some words. To make it easier for you, the words are in three sets. Set 1 consists of ひらがな from the first page of the chart and Set 2 consists of those from the second page. The final challenge is Set 3, which comprises words using ひらがな from the whole chart. See how many symbols/words you can read from memory then use the chart to search for those you cannot remember. Keep coming back to this activity. Try keeping a score of how many words you can read each time and challenge yourself to improve it! Where you have already learnt the 漢字 for a word this is also given in brackets. However, the purpose of this activity is to practise reading ひらがな.

Set 1

a あさ (morning)　**b** て (hand 手)　**c** なつ (summer)
d とけい (clock)　**e** しお (salt)　**f** なに (what)
g ぬの (cloth)

Set 2

a よる (evening)　**b** みみ (ear 耳)　**c** はる (spring)
d ふゆ (winter)　**e** むら (village)　**f** やま (mountain 山)
g もり (forest 森)　**h** わん (bowl)

Set 3

a おはよう (good morning)　**b** きょうなら (goodbye)
c ねこ (cat)　**d** せんせい (teacher)
e いぬ (dog)　**f** め (eye 目)
g へそ (navel)　**h** ひと (person 人)
i れい (example 例)　**j** にほん (Japan 日本)

ⓘ Similar hiragana

You have probably confused some of the similar-looking ひらがな already. This section will line these up and point out the differences to help you keep them separate in your mind. Notice the punctuation, by the way – a comma 、 and a full stop 。 – not all that different from English.

き、さ。	き (ki) has two horizontal lines, さ (sa) has one.
さ、ち。	さ (sa) leans to the left, ち (chi) looks like the number 5 (the top has slipped!)
い、こ。	い (i) is more or less vertical, こ (ko) is horizontal.
い、り。	い (i) – the left stroke is slightly longer than the right, り (ri) – the right stroke is longer than the left.
け、は、ほ。	け (ke) has no loop at the end, は (ha) has only one horizontal line, ほ (ho) has two horizontal lines.
ほ、ま。	The top horizontal line in ほ (ho) sits on top of the vertical line whereas in ま (ma) both horizontal lines cut through the vertical.

す、む。　　　　　す (*su*) curves to the left, む (*mu*) curves to the right and has an extra stroke.

ぬ、め、ね。　　ぬ (*nu*) has two stroke ends at the top and a loop at the bottom whereas め (*me*) has the same stroke ends but no loop, and ね (*ne*) has only one vertical stroke.

る、ろ。　　　　る (*ru*) has a loop, ろ (*ro*) looks a bit like a number 3.

Explanation: Contracted sounds

You have now been introduced to the 46 basic ひらがな symbols. As well as these 46, there are other sounds which are made by combining some of the basic symbols. This is done by combining the symbols which end in the 'i' sound (き、し、ち、に、ひ、み、り) with a small version of や、ゆ、or よ。Each sound is pronounced as a single syllable or 'beat'. Look at the following chart:

き (*ki*) → きゃ (*kya*)	きゅ (*kyu*)	きょ (*kyo*)
し (*shi*) → しゃ (*sha*)	しゅ (*shu*)	しょ (*sho*)
ち (*chi*) → ちゃ (*cha*)	ちゅ (*chu*)	ちょ (*cho*)
に (*ni*) → にゃ (*nya*)	にゅ (*nyu*)	にょ (*nyo*)
ひ (*hi*) → ひゃ (*hya*)	ひゅ (*hyu*)	ひょ (*hyo*)
み (*mi*) → みゃ (*mya*)	みゅ (*myu*)	みょ (*myo*)
り (*ri*) → りゃ (*rya*)	りゅ (*ryu*)	りょ (*ryo*)

練習四　Activity 4

This activity is going to utilize some of the wide range of 'onomatopoeic' words which the Japanese have in their language. These are words which sound like the action or sound word they name. In Japanese, such words usually repeat a sound twice. The nearest English equivalents are phrases such as 'woof woof' for a dog's bark; 'plip plop' for the sound of rain; and 'gobble gobble' for the sound of a turkey but words like this in Japanese are not limited to children's words.

One point to note before you start this activity – many of the words that follow are lengthened by the addition of a vowel sound, normally う (*u*), at the end (but あ (*a*) is also used in these examples). For instance, ちゅうちゅう (a mouse's squeak) is pronounced 'chuu chuu' (usually written 'chū chū' – the line over the vowel represents the additional 'u'). Let one sound run into the other smoothly – do not separate ちゅ (*chu*) and う (*u*).

Now practise reading and saying the following onomatopoeic words. Refer back to the earlier chart to help you as necessary. Two symbols you have learnt previously, ん (n) and ろ (ro) are also used here.

a きゃあきゃあ (scream with laughter)
b しゅんしゅん (fizzing sound)
c しゅうしゅう (fizzing sound)
d ちゅうちゅう (mouse's squeak)
e にゃあにゃあ (miaow)
f ひゅうひゅう (whistling sound)
g ひょろひょろ (swaying; lanky)
h きょろきょろ (looking around)

Explanation: Hiragana that change their sound

You have learnt nearly all the extra rules for ひらがな so you can relax, they are not endless! And also, if you think you have taken in enough at any stage, leave this unit, carry on with the 漢字 units and come back to this later. You are not expected to remember everything in this unit in one go and no one is setting the pace except you!

Some of the ひらがな symbols change their sound with the addition of two small strokes ゛ (ten ten) at the top right of the symbol. Let us look at these:

1 k sounds become g sounds (hard g as in *get*):

か、き、く、け、こ → が、ぎ、ぐ、げ、ご
(ka, ki, ku, ke, ko)　　ga gi gu ge go

2 s sounds → z sounds:

さ、し、す、せ、そ → ざ、じ、ず、ぜ、ぞ
(sa, shi, su, se, so)　　za ji* zu ze zo

* じ is pronounced *ji*.

3 t sounds become d sounds:

た、ち、つ、て、と → だ、(ぢづ) て、ど
(ta, chi, tsu, te, to)　　da (ji zu)* de do

* the sounds ぢ (*ji*) and づ (*zu*) are not normally used because they create the same sound as じ (*ji*) and ず (*zu*). See **2**.

4 *h* sounds become *b* sounds:

は、ひ、ふ、へ、ほ → ば、び、ぶ、べ、ぼ
(*ha*, *hi*, *fu*, *he*, *ho*)   *ba* *bi* *bu* *be* *bo*

5 In addition, *h* sounds become *p* sounds when a small circle °
(*maru*) is added:

は、ひ、ふ、へ、ほ → ぱ、ぴ、ぷ、ぺ、ぽ
(*ha*, *hi*, *fu*, *he*, *ho*)   *pa* *pi* *pu* *pe* *po*

These five sets of rules cover all the sound changes for single
ひらがな symbols. Look over these rules, cover up the *rōmaji*
and try reading them, then try the simple activity that follows.

練習五 Activity 5

Say the sounds out loud or write them down. Refer to the rules
given earlier for the answers.

a ぎ、じ、び、ぴ   b げ、ぜ、て、べ、ぺ
c が、ぎ、だ、ば、ぱ   d ぐ、ず、ぶ、ぷ
e ご、ぞ、ど、ぼ、ぽ

Finally in this section, do you remember the contracted sounds
you learnt on p. 67? Well, the rules just given also apply to
these. The chart that follows groups these sounds on the left.
The *rōmaji* is also given on the right but cover this up and see if
you can work out how to read the ひらがな before you refer to
the *rōmaji*.

ぎゃ、ぎゅ、ぎょ   *gya, gyu, gyo*
じゃ、じゅ、じょ   *ja, ju, jo*
びゃ、びゅ、びょ   *bya, byu, byo*
ぴゃ、ぴゅ、ぴょ   *pya, pyu, pyo*

Explanation: The small つ (*tsu*)

The final rule you need to know in order to read ひらがな
properly is the use of the small つ in a word. When you see this,
you do not pronounce it but pause slightly (a glottal stop) before
saying the next sound. This is shown in *rōmaji* by doubling the
next consonant. The length of this pause is the same as in these
English examples: *headdress* (pause after 'hea', not 'head dress');
and *bookcase* (pause after 'boo'). Here are some Japanese
examples with the *rōmaji* and a pronunciation guide beneath:

a まって (*wait!*)   b きって (*stamp*)   c きっぷ (*ticket*)
   matte   *kitte*   *kippu*
   ma (pause) *te*   *ki* (pause) *te*   *ki* (pause) *pu*

読む練習 Reading practice

Take a deep breath! You are now going to put into practice everything you have learnt in this unit. These initial activities will keep referring you back to the different sections and remember – you can keep revisiting these activities to see if you can improve your score. You do not need to be perfect first time round! Most of these words are usually written with 漢字 but the purpose of the activities that follow is to practise reading ひらがな.

練習六 Activity 6

This activity will use ひらがな from the initial chart (pp. 62–3) and contracted sounds (pp. 67, 69).

See how many of these words you can read.

a きゃく (customer)   b きょう (today)
c ぎゅうにゅう (milk)   d しゃしん (photograph)
e じゃね (See you!)   f ちょうしょく (breakfast)
g ちゅうしょく (lunch)   h ひゃく (100)
i びょういん (hospital)   j りょこう (travel)

練習七 Activity 7

This activity will use ひらがな from the initial chart (pp. 62–3) plus ひらがな which change their sound (pp. 68–9). Once again, see how many of these words you can read.

a みず (water)
b かぎ (keys)
c じてん (dictionary)
d でんわ (telephone)
e たんぽぽ (dandelion)
f どきどき (sound of heart beating fast)
g がぶがぶ (gulping sound – when drinking)

練習八 Activity 8

This activity gives you practice at reading words with the small つ (p. 69).

a ちょっと (a little)   b まって (wait)
c やっぱり (as expected)   d がっこう (school)
e がんばって (Good luck!)   f まっすぐ (straight ahead)

Explanation: Hiragana and kanji

You will already have noticed from the instruction words used throughout this book (and in the last activity) that Japanese is written as a mixture of ひらがな and 漢字 (and カタカナ – *katakana*, introduced in Unit 9). The ひらがな parts of the words have a grammatical function. As mentioned in the Introduction, Japanese children first learn to read and write using only ひらがな. As they learn 漢字 they make their writing more sophisticated by replacing words and parts of words written in ひらがな with 漢字. Although it may seem to be a simpler task to read using ひらがな (rather than having to learn 2000 漢字!) in fact, once you know 漢字, texts become easier to read and scan because 漢字 offer visual clues to the meaning.

練習九　Activity 9

You have learnt that ひらがな has a grammatical function. Now you are going to put this to practice. Below are five of the verbs (action words) you learnt in Unit 4. The ひらがな symbols after each 漢字 serve to show the tense of the verb. ます endings indicate the present or future (for instance, I eat / will eat) and ました indicates the past (I ate). (For those of you who have *Teach Yourself Beginner's Japanese*, verbs are introduced in Unit 8.) The *kunyomi* (*Japanese reading*) is used for single 漢字 verbs with ひらがな endings. In Japanese texts, unfamiliar readings are indicated in ふりがな (*furigana*) which is ひらがな written above, below or beside 漢字 to show the pronunciation.

Now see if you can read these verbs:

a 　た　　　　　　　　　　　た
　　食べます (I eat)　　　食べました (I ate)
b 　の　　　　　　　　　　　の
　　飲みます (I drink)　　飲みました (I drank)
c 　み　　　　　　　　　　　み
　　見ます (I look)　　　　見ました (I looked)
d 　か　　　　　　　　　　　か
　　書きます (I write)　　書きました (I wrote)
e 　はな　　　　　　　　　　はな
　　話します (I talk)　　　話しました (I talked)

練習十　Activity 10

In Unit 4 (p. 50) you worked out the meanings of a set of
Japanese sentences by identifying the key 漢字 words. The same
sentences now follow again, but this time you are going to
practise reading the whole sentence in Japanese. You can do this
now because you have learnt to read ひらがな. The readings
for the 漢字 words or parts of words are given in ふりがな
(*furigana*). Check the English meanings of the sentences by
referring back to Unit 4. Read out aloud!

Grammar note: は、を、に and が have grammar functions
which you will learn more about in Unit 10. When は has this
function it is pronounced *wa* (and when it is used as part of a
word it is pronounced in the usual way as *ha*).

1　女（おんな）の人（ひと）は日本語（にほんご）を学（まな）びました。
2　女（おんな）の子（こ）は土曜日（どようび）に休（やす）みました。
3　男（おとこ）の人（ひと）は月（つき）を見（み）ました。
4　林（はやし）さんは森田（もりた）さんに話（はな）しました。
5　男（おとこ）の子（こ）は馬（うま）が好（す）きです。
6　女（おんな）の人（ひと）は竹（たけ）の子（こ）を食（た）べました。
7　山田（やまだ）さんは車（くるま）を売（う）りました。

終りに　Conclusion

In this unit you have learnt the 46 basic ひらがな symbols plus
related sounds and rules. You have had the chance to write them
and to read words and phrases in ひらがな. You have learnt the
two main uses of ひらがな

- to write words not normally written in 漢字
- to indicate grammar functions and word endings.

You will come across ひらがな again in Unit 10 and you can
refer back to this unit whenever you need to, so do not worry if
you have not taken everything in with the first attempt!

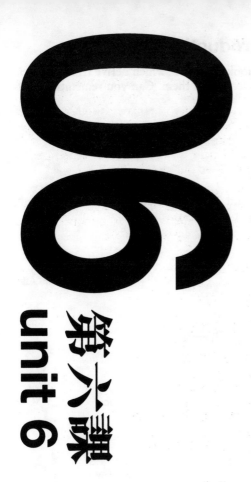

06

unit 6　第六課

In this unit you will
- learn to decode the meanings of 39 new 漢字
- learn to read more compound 漢字 words
- try some activities to review all the 漢字 you have learnt so far
- learn to read and write 11 adjectives (describing words)

はじめに　Introduction

In Units 1 and 2 you looked at 漢字 which derive from pictures of nature. Here is a selection of them. Can you remember their meanings?

a 土　　b 木　　c 女　　d 石
e 口　　f 馬　　g 日　　h 月

Work it out!

As you did in Units 1 and 2, see if you can match the following pictures with the correct 漢字 (a–j).

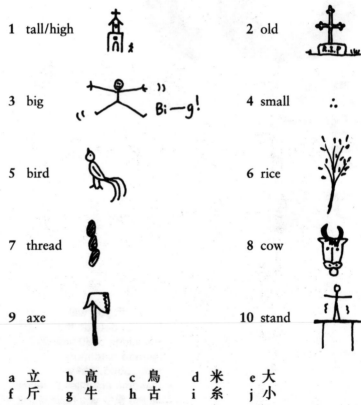

1 tall/high

2 old

3 big

4 small

5 bird

6 rice

7 thread

8 cow

9 axe

10 stand

a 立　　b 高　　c 鳥　　d 米　　e 大
f 斤　　g 牛　　h 古　　i 糸　　j 小

How did you get on? Check your answers at the back and then look at the development sequence from picture to modern kanji that follows.

1　高
tall/high
高 → → → 高

2　古
old
→ 古 → 古

3　大
big
Bi—g! → → 大

4　小
small
→ → 小

5　鳥
bird
→ → 鳥 → 鳥

6　米
rice
→ → → 米

7　糸
thread
→ → → → 糸

8　牛
cow
→ → → 牛

9　斤
axe
→ → 斤

10　立
stand
→ → 立

練習一 Activity 1

Match the 漢字 in the left column with the English meanings in the right column. Look back at the 漢字 pictures if you need to remind yourself of the meanings.

a 牛   1 small
b 斤   2 big
c 高   3 old
d 立   4 tall/high (also means 'expensive')
e 糸   5 bird
f 古   6 cow
g 小   7 rice
h 鳥   8 thread
i 大   9 axe
j 米   10 stand (up)

Explanation: Decoding kanji

About 2–3% of 漢字 derive from simple pictorial representations. As you have already learnt, many of these simple pictorial 漢字 are also used as components in more complex 漢字. You will be looking at this in more detail in Unit 7 but one of the purposes of this unit is to introduce you to some more simple 漢字 which will help you in this unit, and later, to decode the meaning and make-up of other more complex 漢字.

Let us start with four new 漢字 and look at how their components can be brought together into a story to give the meaning.

1 母 (*mother*). You can see the outline of 女 (**woman**) in this

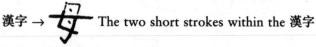

漢字 → The two short strokes within the 漢字

indicate **breasts**, hence *mother*.

2 安 (*cheap, safe*). Again, you can see the 漢字 for **woman**. The component above is like a **hat** or covering. So the 漢字 looks like a **woman** wearing a **cheap hat**!

3 広 (*wide, spacious*). The left side of this 漢字 should remind you of a **cliff** or **cave**.
   Within it is a triangular shape with a **wide** base (it also looks like a **wide nose**!).

4 新 (*new*). You have learnt two of these components in this unit. The top left is 立 (**stand (up)**), the rightside is 斤 (**axe**). The remaining component (bottom left) is 木 (**tree**).
Story: **cut** down a **standing tree** and get **new** wood.

練習二 Activity 2

Now you are going to try to link new 漢字 with stories to establish their meanings. Three of the following 漢字 represent colours (*blue*, *white*, *black*) and the other two mean *father* and *rain*. Which is which? Look at the 漢字, read the stories and link them up.

a 黑　b 白　c 青　d 父　e 雨

1 **Rain.** This 漢字 looks like drops of **rain** against a window.
2 **White.** The components, **sun** (日) and **ray** (short stroke) depict the **white** rays of the sun.
3 **Father.** He has a long moustache and dimples in his cheeks!
4 **Black.** The components, **rice field**, **earth** and **fire** (four short 'flamelike' strokes) depict the deep **black** colour which the earth turns when the rice stubble is burnt after the harvest.
5 **Blue.** This 漢字 also means **green** (for example, the colour of traffic lights and apples). Its components are **earth** with an extra horizontal line which means plants growing out of the ground and **moon**. Young plants are **green** and we speak of a **blue** moon.

練習三 Activity 3

As in Activity 1 you are going to see how well you can remember the 漢字 you have been introduced to in this section (nine in total). Link the 漢字 to the English meaning.

a 安　　　1 father
b 雨　　　2 mother
c 青　　　3 white
d 新　　　4 black
e 広　　　5 blue, green
f 母　　　6 cheap, safe
g 白　　　7 wide, spacious
h 黑　　　8 new
i 父　　　9 rain

Explanation: Abstract kanji

In Unit 3 you learnt the 漢字 for numbers (一、二、三、etc.). These are from a small group of 漢字 which depict abstract ideas using shapes and lines. The 漢字 for the words *above*, *below* and *inside* are formed in a similar way. Look at these 漢字:

1 上 (*above*, *on top*) has a baseline with a 't' shape **above** it.
2 下 (*below*, *under*) has a baseline with a 't' shape **below** it.
3 中 (*inside*, *middle*) is a box with a line through the **middle**.

You can also imagine 上 and 下 to look like the top and roots of a plant.

 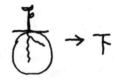

You have now learnt 22 new 漢字 in this unit. Let us review them, grouping them together by theme.

Colours
青 (*blue*)　白 (*white*)　黒 (*black*)

Adjectives (describing words)
大 (*big*)　小 (*small*)　古 (*old*)　新 (*new*)
高 (*tall, expensive*)　安 (*cheap, safe*)　広 (*wide*)

People, animals
母 (*mother*)　父 (*father*)　牛 (*cow*)　鳥 (*bird*)

Nature, basic items
雨 (*rain*)　米 (*rice*)　斤 (*axe*)　糸 (*thread*)

Position
上 (*above*)　下 (*below*)　中 (*inside*)　立 (*stand up*)

Kanji build up: Complex kanji

In Units 2 and 4 you learnt that more complex 漢字 are made from combinations of simpler 漢字. These simpler 漢字 become components of the more complex ones. Examples you have learnt include 男 (*man*), 好 (*like*) and 聞 (*listen*). Now let us look at 漢字 you have learnt in this unit which are also used as components in more complex 漢字.

雨 **Rain** is used as a component of more complex 漢字 to indicate types of weather (with rain as their basis), such as:

雲 **Cloud.** The lower components are *two* and *triangle shape* – think of them as 'two cloud shapes'!

曇 **Cloudy weather.** The lower part is *cloud* and the upper component is 日 (*sun*). Cloudy weather blocks out the sun!

雪 **Snow** ('frozen rain'). The lower component (⊒) looks like 山 (*mountain*) on its side. Think of snow-covered mountains!

雷 **Thunder.** The lower component is *rice field*, a place where farmers would be very aware of thunderstorms.

電 **Electric** is an interesting progression from *thunder*. This time you can see a flash of lightning through the rice field – and lightning creates electricity!

練習四　Activity 4

You are going to try identifying more complex 漢字 by looking at the components and linking them into a meaning. Here are the 漢字:

a	犬	b	島	c	音	d	辛
e	少	f	鳩	g	霜	h	尖

Story meanings

1 *Meaning: island.* Japan is made up of many, many small islands, often just rocky hills in the sea with only birds living on them. This 漢字, therefore, is a depiction of a *bird* sitting (you can't see its tail feathers) on a *mountain*.

2 *Meaning: dove, pigeon.* The components *bird* and *nine* represent a dove.

3 *Meaning: hot/bitter* (taste). The components *stand up* and *ten* combine to give an image of strong flavours which make the taste buds stand up to the power of ten!

4 *Meaning: dog.* The components *big* + short stroke depict a large dog with its tongue hanging out!

5 *Meaning: sound, noise.* Components: *stand up* and *sun.* Stand in the sun and listen to the sounds.

6 *Meaning: pointed, tapered.* Components *big* and *small.* Put simply, tapering to a point involves something becoming smaller.

7 *Meaning: few, a little.* Components: *small* and a diagonal stroke.

8 *Meaning: frost.* Components: *rain, tree* and *eye.* Frost (made from rain) on trees looks like millions of sparkling eyes.

Finally, the 漢字 for *fat* is 太. This looks very similar to 犬 (*dog*). You can distinguish them by thinking of the short stroke in *dog* as the tongue and of the short stroke in *fat* as a marker indicating the widest or fattest part of the 漢字.

In this section of kanji build up you have been introduced to 14 new 漢字. They are listed here. Can you remember their meanings? Check back through the section if there are any you are unsure about.

雪、雲、電、雷、霜、曇、犬、太、少、辛、音、尖、鳩、島。

Kanji build up: Kanji compounds 1

Remember that kanji compounds are words created from two or more 漢字. You have come across examples of these in Units 1–4. Words such as 人口 (*population*), 日曜日 (*Sunday*) and 食物 (*food*) are some of the 漢字 compounds you have learnt so far.

The next two activities are designed to get you thinking about the meanings of some new 漢字 words using the 漢字 you have been introduced to in this unit plus others you have learnt in earlier units.

練習五　Activity 5

This activity uses combinations of 漢字 you have learnt in this unit only. Match the two 漢字 words in the box with the English meanings from the list beneath it.

a　白鳥	b　大雨	c　父母	d　青白
e　小犬	f　小牛	g　広大	h　白米

Meanings
1 vast　2 swan　3 calf　4 puppy, small dog　5 parents
6 polished (white) rice　7 pale; blue-white　8 heavy rain

練習六　Activity 6

This activity combines 漢字 from this unit with some you have learnt from previous units. Those from previous units are:

年 (*year*)、学 (*study*)、女 (*woman*)、車 (*vehicle*)、手 (*hand*)、人 (*person*)、口 (*mouth*)、目 (*eye*)、聞 (*listen*)、話 (*talk*)、中 (*middle*)

Again, choose the appropriate 漢字 word from the box to match its English meaning. The bracketed information gives the literal meaning in cases where the meaning may not be immediately obvious.

a	新年	b	青年	c	少年	d	少女	e	大学
f	小人	g	大人	h	糸口	i	年上	j	目上
k	上手	l	下手	m	新車	n	新聞	o	電車
p	電話	q	中古車						

1 university (*big study*)
2 train (*electric vehicle*)
3 good at (*upper hand*)
4 bad at (*lower hand*)
5 youth (*blue years = innocence*)
6 your superiors (their *eye level* is *above you*)
7 child (*small person*)
8 adult (*big person*)
9 clue (*the thread mouth!*)
10 telephone (*electric talk*)
11 new year
12 older {than you} *years above*)
13 boy (*few years*)
14 girl (*a few / a little bit a woman*)
15 new car
16 second-hand car (*in the middle of being old*)
17 newspaper (*newly heard*)

Check your answers before moving on to the next section.

Kanji build up: Kanji compounds 2

Finally in this section, you are going to extend your knowledge of 漢字 compounds a little further by learning three new 漢字 and looking at how these are used in combination with 漢字 you have learnt in this unit to make new words.

1 国 means *country* and is the depiction of a king (玉 *lit. jewel*) within the boundaries (囗) of his kingdom. Examples of its usage are:

米国 'rice country' is the Japanese word for *America*. (The rice grown in America is short-grained like Japanese rice and often packaged and sold as Japanese rice.)

中米 'middle rice' is the Japanese word for *Central America*.

中国 'middle country' means *China* (the central country of Asia).

母国 *Mother country* means exactly that, the country you originate from.

島国 *Island country* (such as Japan, Britain and Australia).

2 肉 means *meat* or *flesh*. You can see two people (人) hanging from a frame!

　　牛肉 'cow meat' means *beef*.
　　鳥肉 'bird meat' means *chicken*.

3 校 means *school*. The left side, *tree* (木) indicates a wooden building (Japanese schools were traditionally made of wood) and the right side is *father* (父) wearing a hat. Think of this as a teacher.

　　学校　　　'study school' means *school*.
　　小学校　　'small school' means *elementary* or *primary school*.
　　中学校　　means *middle school* or *junior high school*.
　　高校　　　means *high school* (abbreviated version of 高等学校).

練習七　Activity 7

In this unit you have been introduced to 36 new 漢字 compounds. You can see them all in the following list and your task is to test your memory by writing the meanings in the brackets after each word. Then check your answers by looking back through the previous sections.

白鳥 (　　)	大雨 (　　)	父母 (　　)	青白 (　　)
小犬 (　　)	小牛 (　　)	広大 (　　)	白米 (　　)
新年 (　　)	青年 (　　)	少年 (　　)	少女 (　　)
大学 (　　)	小人 (　　)	大人 (　　)	糸口 (　　)
年上 (　　)	目上 (　　)	上手 (　　)	下手 (　　)
新車 (　　)	新聞 (　　)	米国 (　　)	中米 (　　)
中国 (　　)	母国 (　　)	島国 (　　)	牛肉 (　　)
鳥肉 (　　)	学校 (　　)	小学校 (　　)	中学校 (　　)
高校 (　　)	電車 (　　)	電話 (　　)	中古車 (　　)

Kanji readings

In this section you are going to learn to say the 11 adjectives (describing words), learnt in this unit, in Japanese. Look up the *kunyomi* (*Japanese reading*) for the following 漢字 in the unit chart at the back of the book.

高、安、小、大、少*、古、新、太、広、白

* 少 has two *kunyomi* – *sukuna(i)* means *few*; *suko(shi)* means *a little*.

Notice that part of the reading is written in brackets. This is the part which is written in ひらがな. For example: *taka(i)* is written 高い meaning: *tall, expensive*.

Memorize the whole reading including the part in brackets then try the activity that follows.

練習八 Activity 8

You are now going to practise reading the 11 adjectives as complete words including the ひらがな endings. Even if you have not yet worked through Unit 5, you can still do this because the whole word is given in the unit chart. And the answers are given at the back of the book.

a 高い b 安い c 小さい d 大きい
e 少い f 少し g 古い h 新しい
i 太い j 広い k 白い

書く練習五 Writing practice 5

In Units 1 and 2 you learnt some general rules for writing 漢字. You put these into practice in Unit 3 to write 漢字 numbers and in Unit 4 to write 漢字 verbs. Now you are going to learn to write the ten 漢字 from Activity 8 in this unit. Use squared paper and focus on the proportions and overall balance of each 漢字. Once you feel confident, see if you can write them from memory. Keep saying the meaning (and the readings) to yourself as you write them to help fix all the different elements into your memory.

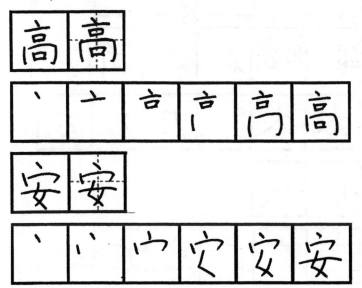

大	大	一	ナ	大
小	小	亅	小	小
少	少	亅	小	小	少
古	古	一	十	古
新	新
丶	丷	十	立	立
亲	亲	新	新	新
太	太	一	ナ	大	太
広	広
丶	亠	广	広	広

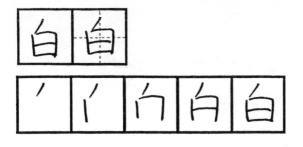

終りに　Conclusion

In this unit you have been introduced to a total of 39 single 漢字 through picture association and through analysing their component parts. You have also learnt 36 new 漢字 compounds and have practised reading and writing the 漢字 words for 11 adjectives. Units 1–6 have altogether introduced you to 97 single 漢字, 100 漢字 compounds (including 13 surnames) and the whole ひらがな syllabary! おめでとう (*omedetō*) Congratulations! Of course, you might not remember all or even most of these but the purpose of this book is to help you understand more about Japanese script, about how it is made up and to find ways for you to break the 漢字 code and to build on your learning. Even Japanese people forget 漢字 from time to time; it takes time and practice to build up your knowledge of them. But remember – Japanese script can be fun to learn too!

テスト　Test

a The test at the end of Unit 4 contained a summary of all the single 漢字 you had learnt up to that point. This activity pulls together all the single 漢字 you have learnt in this unit. Can you identify them all? They are in ascending order of stroke number. The answers are at the back but do not worry if you can not do them all on the first attempt – you can keep coming back to this activity!

1 上	2 下	3 小	4 大	5 中	6 犬
7 太	8 少	9 斤	10 父	11 牛	12 立
13 古	14 母	15 広	16 白	17 米	18 安
19 糸	20 尖	21 肉	22 辛	23 雨	24 青
25 国	26 音	27 高	28 島	29 校	30 黒
31 鳥	32 雪	33 雲	34 新	35 雷	36 電
37 鳩	38 曇	39 霜			

b This activity is designed to test how well you remember the compound words you have learnt so far. The surnames are not included, you can review these by turning to Activity 7 of Unit 2. The words below are grouped by theme (loosely in some cases!). What do they mean in English?

Days of the week
1 日曜日 2 土曜日 3 水曜日
4 火曜日

School and study
5 入学 6 小学校 7 中学校
8 高校 9 休学 10 見学

Countries
11 日本 12 中国 13 米国
14 中米 15 母国 16 島国

Food and drink
17 牛肉 18 鳥肉 19 食物
20 飲物 21 白米 22 飲水

Transport
23 電車 24 新車 25 中古車
26 馬車 27 人力車

Animals
28 小犬 29 小牛 30 白鳥

People
31 父母 32 小人 33 大人
34 少年 35 少女 36 女子

Shopping and travel
37 買物 38 見物 39 入口
40 出口 41 休日

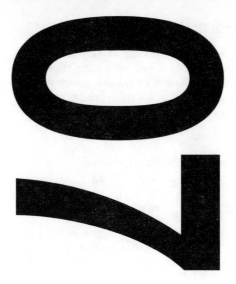

07

第七課
unit 7

In this unit you will
- learn about the different types of 漢字
- learn more about 漢字 radicals and components
- identify 漢字 meanings from their radical
- learn to write 漢字 in the correct proportions

はじめに　Introduction

In Units 2, 4 and 6 you looked at how simpler 漢字 are used as components of more complex ones. Look back over these units if you find now or later that you need to refresh your memory. In this unit you are going to look in more depth at ways you can crack the code for more complex 漢字. First of all you are going to test your memory of some of the complex 漢字 you have learnt so far.

1　What are the meanings of the 漢字 that follow?

a 林　　b 森　　c 男　　d 好　　e 明　　f 聞
g 見　　h 書　　i 言　　j 売　　k 読　　l 話
m 買　　n 休　　o 出　　p 学

2　What are the meanings of the left sides of the 漢字 in this list? (You will not know the whole meaning at this stage.) Refer to p. 44 if you need more information about the left side of a.

a 体　　b 唱　　c 埋　　d 妹　　e 孫　　f 時
g 肘　　h 村　　i 畑　　j 町　　k 眠　　l 談
m 針　　n 転

Explanation: Types of kanji

There are a number of ways in which 漢字 have been developed. You are already familiar with the first three of these categories:

1　Pictorial kanji

These fairly simple 漢字 derive from pictures of nature. Examples are 山 (*mountain*), 川 (*river*) and 人 (*person*). They make up about 2–3% of all 漢字.

2　Simple abstract kanji

These 漢字 convey abstract ideas through symbols, for example, the numbers (Unit 3). There are only a very few of this kind.

3　Complex pictorial kanji

These are made up of two or more basic pictorial 漢字 which together convey a new meaning. Examples are 林 (*wood*), 男 (*man*) and 明 (*bright*) but Activity 2 in the introduction to this unit has more examples which you will be learning. Again, this type of 漢字 makes up about 2–3% of all 漢字.

4   Sound and meaning kanji

Part of the 漢字 conveys the general meaning and part conveys the pronunciation (*onyomi* or Chinese reading). By identifying the component parts you have a clue to the meaning and how to say it. Examples (from Introduction, Activity 2) include 時 (*time*) and 転 (*turn*). About 90% of 漢字 belong to this group.

This unit is going to focus on categories 3 and 4 and you are going to learn ways of cracking the 漢字 code!

Explanation: Kanji components

As you have already learnt, more complex 漢字 are made up of simpler ones which we have called components. One of these components, known as the **radical**, often gives a clue to the general meaning of the whole 漢字. Many radicals are themselves 漢字, usually of the simple pictorial kind. In dictionaries, 漢字 are grouped by their radical (same radical, same group). You will learn more about this later in the unit.

In Activity 2 of the introduction to this unit, you identified the left part of each 漢字. You were, in fact, identifying the radical in this activity – the most common location of a radical is on the left side of a 漢字. There are in total 214 radicals according to the traditional Chinese classification. The purpose of this unit is to introduce you to a few of the more common radicals and to make you familiar with the idea of radicals so that you have a solid foundation to build on.

練習一   Activity 1

In this activity you will have a go at identifying new 漢字 (a–l below) which are formed by combining two or more pictorial 漢字 (category 3 on p. 88). You have already come across some of these new 漢字 in Activity 2 of the introduction to this unit. Beneath a–l are a number of stories and meanings. See if you can match each 漢字 with a story and meaning by looking at the components that make up the 漢字.

a 信	b 唱	c 畑	d 談	e 孫	f 鳴
g 語	h 炎	i 焚	j 埋	k 旦	l 姦

Stories and meanings

1 **Three women** together are very wicked! *Meaning: wickedness.*

2 Heaping **fire** upon **fire** creates a blaze. *Meaning: blaze, flame.*

3 A **fire** burning **wood** (**two trees**). *Meaning: burn, kindle.*

4 A **field** burnt by **fire** is ready for cultivation. *Meaning: cultivated field.*

5 The **mouth** of the **bird** creates birdsong. *Meaning: cry, chirp (of birds, animals).*

6 A **person's words** are to be believed. *Meaning: believe.*

7 The **three mouths** (the **lines in two** look like tongues) chanted in unison. *Meaning: chant, recite.*

8 They dug up the **rice field** and buried the treasure in the **earth beneath**. *Meaning: be buried.*

9 The visual image is 'speaking **fiery words**'. *Meaning: discussion, conversation.*

10 'Speaking **five mouths**'. In other words, five languages. *Meaning: language(s).*

11 The **sun** rising above the **horizon**. *Meaning: dawn.*

12 The **child** is attached to its ancestors by a genetic **thread** (there is a **short line** above the thread which is attached to the child). *Meaning: grandchild.*

Explanation: More about radicals and components

In the last activity you arrived at the meaning of the 漢字 by linking the components into a story. You can do this with many 漢字 and even though sometimes the story or link may seem far-fetched, if the meanings of the components are kept consistent, this method can be a very useful code-breaker and memory 'jog' when learning new 漢字.

You have already learnt in this unit that the radical of a 漢字 usually conveys its general meaning. Let us look at this in more detail using the radical 言 (*say*). Some 漢字 follow which contain this radical (on the left side):

記 (*narrative, history*)   訳 (*translation*)
証 (*proof, certificate*)   調 (*tune*)
談 (*conversation*)   詩 (*poem*)
語 (*language*)   課 (*lesson*)

These examples show that the radical indicates a general link with the meaning of speech or words (including musical 'words' or notes in the case of 調 – *tune*). Now let us look at some of the more common radicals. Remember there are 214 altogether but the aim of this unit is to introduce you to the idea of radicals and to show you ways in which they can be helpful in learning 漢字.

Here are the left-hand radicals which you identified in Activity 2 (introduction). You learnt the meanings in earlier units.

> 人 (*person*)　口 (*mouth*)　土 (*earth*)
> 女 (*woman*)　日 (*sun, day*)　子 (*child*)
> 月 (*moon*)　木 (*tree*)　火 (*fire*)
> 田 (*rice field*)　目 (*eye*)　言 (*say; words*)
> 金 (*gold, metal* – as a radical it normally means *metal*)
> 車 (*car, vehicle*, also *wheel*)

You have already learnt that a 漢字 may change shape slightly when used as a radical. Here are some examples (the radical is on the left):

1 Radicals may appear 'squashed'　埋 (radical = *earth*)
2 Radicals may have some shorter strokes　林 (radical = *tree*)
3 Radicals may change their shape　体 (radical = *person*)

Here are two more useful radicals whose shape differs from the 漢字 you have met already:

水 (*water*) as a left-hand radical → 泊 (looks like three splashes of water)

手 (*hand*) as a left-hand radical → 折 (squashed and the top line has gone)

One more point to note before you begin the next activity is that two of the radicals already mentioned have two meanings. They are:

月 (*moon*) but this has the second meaning *flesh* (from a 'squashed' version of 肉 – *flesh/meat*)

日 (*sun*) but can also take the meaning *speak* (from 曰 (*to speak*) – 'a tongue in a mouth' – although this is rare)

練習二　Activity 2

In this activity you will look at a number of 漢字 with the radical missing. The meaning of the full 漢字 is given (plus a story where appropriate) and you have to decide which radical (from those listed above) will complete the 漢字 (the answers are on the next page). Here is an example to help you:

舌 *Components*: **tongue** and **mouth**. *Story*: you must drink water to live. *Meaning*: *to live*. Answer: 活 (radical = *water*).

a 本 *Components*: **root** (of tree). *Story*: the root/origin of a person is their body. *Meaning*: *body*.

b 丁 *Component*: a **marker** or **post**. *Story*: rice fields mark a town's boundaries. *Meaning*: *town*.

c 寸 *Component*: **measurement**. *Story*: the villagers measured and cut wood to make their homes. *Meaning*: *village*.

d 未 *Components*: tree and short top branches = not yet (that is, not yet a fully-grown tree) *Story*: someone who is not yet a woman. *Meaning*: *younger sister*.

e 丁 *Component*: a **marker or post**. *Story*: fire on a post makes a lamp to mark your way. *Meaning*: *lamp*.

f 斤 *Component*: **axe**. *Story*: with his hand he wielded the axe to break the object. *Meaning*: *break, snap, fold*.

g 民 *Component*: **people, nation**. *Story*: the people closed their eyes and slept. *Meaning*: *sleep*.

h 犬 *Component*: **dog**. *Story*: dogs bark with their mouths. *Meaning*: *bark*.

i 寸 *Component*: **measurement**. *Story*: part of the body (flesh) used as an old measurement, from elbow to fingertip. *Meaning*: *elbow*.

j 白 *Component*: **white**. *Story*: the hotel we stayed at had water and clean white towels. *Meaning*: *stay at*.

k 十 *Component*: **ten**, but imagine it to be a needle with thread coming out of it (horizontal line). *Story*: needles are made of metal. *Meaning*: *needle*.

l 二 + ム *Components*: **two** (+ a shape which looks like a nose! In the 漢字 the two is above the nose). *Story*: the car's two wheels rotate. *Meaning*: *to rotate, turn*.

m 寺 *Components*: **earth** and **measurement** = **temple** (think of the Buddhist priests plotting out the area of land before building the temple). *Story*: the temple bell struck each hour all through the day. *Meaning*: *time, hour*.

How did you get on? Here are the 漢字 you have identified, complete with their radical and meaning. Think about how the radical gives a clue to the general meaning and how you can fit the components together into a story.

a 体 (*body*) b 町 (*town*) c 村 (*village*)
d 妹 (*younger sister*) e 灯 (*lamp*) f 折 (*fold, snap*)
g 眠 (*sleep*) h 吠 (*bark*) i 肘 (*elbow*)
j 泊 (*stay at*) k 針 (*needle*) l 転 (*turn*)
m 時 (*time*)

練習三　Activity 3

In Activity 2 in the introduction to this unit you identified the left-hand radicals of 漢字 but not the full meaning. You have now come across all these meanings so turn back to Activity 2 on page 88, and see if you can identify all the 漢字. The answers are in Activities 1 and 2 (pp. 89, 91).

Explanation: Locating the radical

So far you have identified radicals on the left side of 漢字. This is the most common position of a radical but not the only one. Here are the other locations with examples (the radical is in brackets).

Right side	形 *shape* (彡)	都 *capital* (阝)	
Above	茶 *tea* (艹)	安 *cheap* (宀)	
Below	楽 *enjoyable* (木)	急 *emergency* (心)	
Surround – complete	国 *country* (囗)		
Surround – partial	店 *shop* (广)	道 *road, way* (辶)	
	聞 *listen* (門)		

Some radicals are located in more than one position. For example, 木 (*tree*) is found:

1　**left side** (林 *woods*)
2　**above** (査 *investigate*)
3　**below** (楽 *enjoy*)

And in different positions, some radicals change their shape. For example, 火 (*fire*):

1　**left side** 畑 (*field*)
2　**below** 煮 (*boil*) Here it looks like four small flames.

And 心 (*heart*):

1　**left side** 情 (*feeling*)
2　**below** 急 (*emergency*)

練習四　Activity 4

The box on the next page contains some common radicals found in the **right-hand**, **above**, **below** or **surround** positions. Their names/meanings are given in brackets.

⺿ (vegetation)	欠 (yawn)	气 (vapour)
阝 (village)	亠 (lid)	宀 (hat!)
	冖 (cover)	火 or 灬 (fire)
⺮ (bamboo)	囗 (enclosure)	穴 (hole)
雨 (rain)		⺖ or 心 (heart)

Look at the 漢字 a–m that follow and decide: **1 which is its radical** (from the box) and **2 its location**. Here is an example to help you. Think as well how the radical may indicate the general meaning.

例 *Rei* 芋 (*potato*)   1   vegetation radical
                        2   above   (link: a potato is a vegetable)

a 安 (*cheap*)	b 花 (*flower*)
c 京 (*capital city*)	d 都 (*large city*)
e 図 (*picture, diagram*)	f 歌 (*song*)
g 筆 (*writing brush*)	h 黒 (*black*)
i 空 (*air, sky*)	j 軍 (*army*)
k 気 (*spirit*)	l 思 (*think*)
m 雪 (*snow*)	

Explanation: Kanji readings

It has already been mentioned earlier on in this unit that as well as the radical often giving the general meaning of 漢字, the other component(s) sometimes indicate the reading (*onyomi*). Below are six 漢字 whose right sides (or in the case of *temple* the whole 漢字) are all the same and are read either *JI* or *SHI*.

寺 (*temple*) *JI*   時 (*time*) *JI*   持 (*hold*) *JI*
侍 (*samurai*) *JI*   峙 (*tower, soar*) *JI*   詩 (*poem*) *SHI*

Notice how the left side (the radical) gives a clue to the meaning. We have discussed some already, for example, 詩 (*poem*) has the radical 言 (*say, words*). 持 (*hold*) has the radical 手 (*hand* – remember it changes its shape slightly). Look at the radicals of the others and think about how these give a pointer to their meaning. (The radical for temple is *earth*.)

練習五　Activity 5

This activity gets you to look at 漢字 whose right sides and *onyomi* reading are the same. You will first be given the right side (this can stand alone as a 漢字 too) and then will choose from a selection of radicals (the full 漢字 is also given in brackets) which radical gives the full 漢字 its particular meaning. Refer to pp. 91, 93–4 if you cannot remember the meaning of a radical. The first one has the answers immediately after, to help you get started.

Right side: 召　(SHŌ)　**Meaning:** call, send for, summon

Radicals (漢字)		Meanings	
a	手　(招)	i beckon, invite	( )
b	日　(昭)	ii inherit	( )
c	水　(沼)	iii imperial edict, decree	( )
d	糸　(紹)	iv clear, bright	( )
e	言　(詔)	v swamp, marsh	( )

Answers

i = a = 招 (link: beckon with your hand)
ii = d = 紹 (link: inheritance 'thread' to relatives)
iii = e = 詔 (link: spoken 'summons' = decree)
iv = b = 昭 (link: sun and bright)
v = c = 沼 (link: swamps are watery)

ℹ Before you try the activity

Look at the example above.

• Sometimes the right-side meaning can be clearly included in the link (as in i–iii); sometimes it is not quite so clear (as in iv and v).
• The radicals are given in their full 漢字 form but they may change shape when used as part of a 漢字 (as in i and v).

1　Right side: 青 (*SEI*)　Meaning: *blue*

Radicals	(漢字)	Meanings	
a	心 (*heart*) (情)	i purify, cleanse	( )
b	日　(晴)	ii request, ask	( )
c	水　(清)	iii spirit/white rice/purity	( )
d	言　(請)	iv fine weather, clear up	( )
e	米 (*rice*) (精)	v feeling, emotion	( )

2 Right side: 乍 (SAKU) No meaning

Radicals		(漢字)	Meanings	
a	日	(昨)	i yesterday, previous	( )
b	人	(作)	ii make, create	( )
c	火	(炸)	iii vinegar	( )
d	酉 (liquid, alcohol)	(酢)	iv explosion	( )

3 Right side: 干 (KAN) Meaning: get dry, parch

Radicals		(漢字)	Meanings	
a	手	(扞)	i wickedness, mischief	( )
b	女	(奸)	ii liver	( )
c	水	(汗)	iii perspire	( )
d	月 (flesh)	(肝)	iv snore	( )
e	鼻 (nose)	(鼾)	v pole, rod	( )
f	竹	(竿)	vi restrain	( )
g	日	(旱)	vii drought, dry weather	( )

Explanation: Using kanji dictionaries

How did you get on in the last activity? It is important to restate at this stage that although many 漢字 have a part which gives a clue to the reading (of the *onyomi*) and that the radical often gives a clue to the general meaning, they do not all fall into these categories. However, remember, you can really begin to make inroads into your learning of 漢字 when you have some rules and clues like this to help you.

Knowing about radicals does become essential when you start to use a 漢字 dictionary. As you learnt in the introduction, the Japanese Ministry of Education made a list of 1942 漢字 which are essential to know in everyday communication. However, there are many more 漢字 than this which are used in specialist, academic and pre-war writings and documents. (Compare this situation with the many more words in an English dictionary than most people know or use in everyday life.) A 漢字 dictionary, therefore, may have 5000 or more entries but many of these are not in common usage.

The most commonly used 漢字 dictionary for non-Japanese people is the *Japanese–English Character Dictionary* by Andrew Nelson (but often referred to simply as 'Nelson'). 漢字 are traditionally looked up in a dictionary by first identifying the radical and then locating the section where all 漢字 with this radical are grouped. Radicals are ordered by their number of strokes from those of one stroke through to those of 16/17 (in Nelson). The number and type of radical does vary slightly from dictionary to dictionary. In Nelson each radical is numbered (from 1–214) and its number is clearly printed at the top of every page so that it is easy to turn to the section you are looking for. There is a list of all the radicals with their number in the inside front cover.

Once you have identified the radical and turned to the relevant section, you next count the number of remaining strokes in the 漢字 you are looking up, excluding the radical stroke number. All 漢字 with the same radical are grouped according to the number of remaining strokes, from 1 through to the highest number (this can be up to 24 or more in the case of very complicated 漢字). As an extra guide, on the side of every page, the radical on that page is given in square brackets with the number of remaining strokes *grouped on the same page* printed next to it. For example:

 tells you that on this page are 漢字 with the radical 木 and four remaining strokes.

Here are the steps for looking up a 漢字 (using Nelson). You want to find the meaning of 枝:

1 You identify the radical (木).
2 Count the number of its strokes (four).
3 Turn to the radical list in the inside cover, find 木 in the 4-stroke group and make a note of its number (75).
4 Turn to section 75 (radical numbers are labelled at the top of each page).
5 Count the number of remaining strokes in 枝 (four).

6 Find the sub-section containing all 漢字 with four remaining strokes (quick reference at the side of each page).
7 Run your eye down the 漢字 listed until you find 枝. ***Meaning: branch.***

If you know the pronunciation of the 漢字 you can look it up in the index at the back. Look through all 漢字 of the same reading until you see the one you want. There is a number next to it (every 漢字 is given its own number). Find this number by looking at the bottom edge of each page.

These steps are to help you get started if you want to use a 漢字 dictionary. Identifying the radical is not always easy (Nelson lists a series of steps at the beginning of the dictionary to assist you) and at the beginning you are bound to make mistakes in counting the number of strokes. But practice makes perfect (!) and with time and experience you will be able to master looking up even very complicated 漢字. You can now see one reason why writing 漢字 correctly is so important – so that you can count how many strokes there are!

If you have access to a 漢字 dictionary, start by looking up the 漢字 you have been introduced to in this unit because the radical has already been identified for you.

書く練習六　Writing practice 6

This is the last formal teaching section for writing in this book (although in Unit 10 you will be taught techniques for letter writing). This writing section is going to focus on the balance between the components of 漢字 (this has already been mentioned in Units 4 and 6). The 漢字 that follow have left sides which you are already familiar with as separate 漢字 but which change their shape slightly when used as radicals. Copy the models carefully and notice changes in size, proportion and orientation of the radical. Look carefully at the way the whole 漢字 is written and do not let the different components divide and look like separate 漢字. As a rule of thumb, where there is a left and right side, the left side takes up one-third and the right side two-thirds.

The 漢字 you are going to learn to write are: 時 (*time*), 畑 (*cultivated field*), 村 (*village*), 泊 (*stay*), 針 (*needle*), 転 (*turn*), 妹 (*younger sister*), 埋 (*bury*) and 気 (*spirit*).

時	時

l	几	月	日	日一

日十	日士	日士	時	時

畑	畑

、	・	・	火	火

火冂	火田	畑	畑

村	村

一	十	オ	木	木一

村	村

妹	妹		
く	女	女	女
女	奸	妹	妹

埋	埋			
一	十	士	打	切
坦	坦	坤	埋	埋

気	気			
ノ	仁	上	気	気	気

終りに Conclusion

In this unit you have covered more than 70 漢字 and 38 of the 214 radicals. However, the purpose of this unit was to introduce you to a technique of breaking down 漢字 into their component parts in order to extract meaning. Therefore, you are not expected to remember all the 漢字 which you have analysed during this unit. More important is the method you have been introduced to for decoding 漢字. The unit chart at the back, therefore, will not include all the 漢字 from this unit, but those learnt in Activities 1 and 2 will be included for reference purposes.

Units 8, 9 and 10 will build on the knowledge and techniques that you have acquired from the first seven units of this book. Unit 8 covers general signs and information notices that you would see if you went to Japan; Unit 9 teaches カタカナ (katakana) the script for non-Japanese words; and Unit 10 offers you the chance to read a variety of Japanese texts. You could take these units in any order – Unit 8, for example, teaches a large number of signs and so you might wish to 'dip into' that unit and then move on and return to it at a later date. It is up to you – you take control of your learning and if you find that something is difficult, or you just want a change, then move on to another unit.

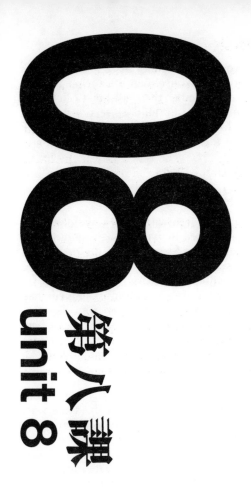

08

第八課 unit 8

In this unit you will
- learn to read everyday signs and written information
- find clues and stories to help you remember new 漢字 words
- learn to recognize different writing styles
- decipher authentic everyday street signs and information

About this unit

You will be introduced to a large number of 漢字 signs in this unit with lots of clues to help you remember them. You are certainly not expected to remember them all but to help you progress through this unit, the kanji build up sections contain additional 漢字 words which you can leave out or come back to later if you find there is already enough new information to take in.

はじめに　Introduction

When we travel around places, even within our own local area, we are constantly being informed by written signs and notices all around us. We pick out the information of use or interest ('sale', 'no entry', 'closed', 'danger') and scan over the information we do not require. Visitors to Japan with no knowledge of written Japanese are struck almost immediately by the lack of information they are able to get from the signs and notices around them. There is some information in English, particularly in larger cities such as Tokyo, but your experience of Japan will be so much richer if you can understand some of the information that is written in Japanese.

When children first learn to read they will obsessively read out all the shop names and road signs they see. In the same way, once you can recognize some of the common signs in Japanese, your eyes will feast on the new source of information open to you. Neon signs, advertisements, shop notices, tourist places, signs at stations – you find yourself able to operate much more efficiently and with more confidence because you can pick out the information you need and get to the places you want to go to.

This and the next unit will introduce you to some of the more common signs you may see around you in Japan. And not only in Japan – television programmes and films often show neon lights and other signs written in Japanese which, once you have completed this book, you can have a go at reading. And in Japanese department stores, restaurants and other speciality shops in large cities outside Japan you see many signs and information written in Japanese. So there are plenty of opportunities to practise what you are going to learn in this unit.

Work it out!

First of all you are going to try reading some common signs which you have already learnt in previous units. The 漢字 words that follow have a box of English meanings beneath them (with clues and stories in brackets where necessary). Can you match them up?

a 入口	b 出口	c 女	d 男	e 上り
f 下り	g 電車	h 大人	i 小人	j お寺
k 学校	l 入国	m 出国	n 千円	o 休日

1 immigration (enter a country)	8 holiday
2 train (electric vehicle)	9 emigration (exit a country)
3 child (small person)	10 adult (big person)
4 entrance	11 school
5 up*	12 exit
6 1000 yen	13 down*
7 men	14 women
	15 temple

The answers in the back also have in brackets the number of the unit where the word was first introduced so that you can look it up again if you need to.

* A quick note about 上り (*up*) and 下り (*down*): these signs are used specifically on trains. 'Up' trains are travelling to Tokyo (from any direction) and 'down' trains are travelling away from Tokyo.

Explanation: Kanji for places

There are a number of 漢字 which are used to indicate different types of places such as shops, rooms, public institutions and offices. Let us look at seven key ones. They are:

1 店 (*shop*)	2 屋 (*store, roof*)
3 局 (*bureau, office*)	4 所 (*place*)
5 場 (*place*)	6 館 (*hall, large building*)
7 園 (*garden*)	

Now let us look at each one in more detail.

1 店 (*shop*). The radical for this is 广 which means *dotted cliff* (厂 means *cliff*). Both these radicals indicate some type of

enclosure. Think of it in this case as the roof and back wall of the shop. The front wall is, of course, a window and so is open. Inside the shop is 卜 (*fortune*) and 口 (*mouth*), together meaning 占 (*fortune telling*). To run a shop you have to be good at divining the customer's needs!

2 屋 (*store, roof*). The radical is 尸 meaning *flag*. Within it is 至 (*arrive*) which has within it 土 (*earth*). The flag is a banner advertising a newly built store (earth connection!), waiting for the customers to arrive!

3 局 (*bureau, office*). The radical again is 尸 (*flag*) and within it is a mouth or opening enclosed on two sides. This 漢字 is used in words such as 'post office' so think of it as the glass counter behind which the office clerk sits. The 'flag' is the board calling the next customer!

4 and 5 所 and 場 (*place*). 所 is generally used to indicate an office or 'over-the-counter' type of place (tourist information office, foreign exchange bureau) whereas 場 has the general meaning *grounds* (hence 土 – *earth* – as the radical). The radical for 所 is 戶 (*flag* with 'one' above it) and this by itself means *door*. You came across the right side in the previous unit, 斤 meaning *axe*. (Use the axe on the door to mark the spot or place!)

6 館 (*hall, large building*). This 漢字 is often used in public or government buildings. You should recognize the left side. It is the radical version of 食 (*food*). The right side 官 has the general meaning of *government*. Put together, large halls (such as concert halls, art galleries) are often funded by local government and you can usually buy refreshments too!

7 園 (*garden*). This 漢字 is very easy to remember! First, there is the radical which you have already come across in the previous unit – 囗 which means *enclosure* or, in this case, the walls around a garden. Within the walls there is 土 (*earth* – think of flower beds!), 口 (*mouth* – but think of this as a pond!) and off the 'pond' are a number of garden paths. Can you see it now?

練習一 Activity 1

Now let us put what you have learnt so far into practice. Some 漢字 which you have already learnt follow. The English meaning is in brackets and, remember, if you want to review a 漢字 at any time, look up the English word in the index and it will refer you back to the page where you first learnt it. There are also some new 漢字 with some tips on how to remember them. Here are the 漢字:

売 (*sell*)　書 (*write*)　本 (*book*)　八百 (*800*)　肉 (*meat*)
飲 (*drink*) 車 (*vehicle*) 手 (*hand*)

美術　*art* (the first 漢字 looks like an artist's easel!).
市　　*city, market* (woman in hat holding shopping bags).
工　　*construction* (looks like scaffolding or tower).
公　　*public* (八 *eight* + ム looks like a nose! Eight nosey people = the public!).
図　　*drawing, map* (囗 is the *picture frame*, the inside is modern art).
魚　　*fish* (components: *hook*, *rice field*, *fire*. The fish is hooked, cooked on fire, eaten with rice).
酒　　*rice wine, alcohol* (*water* radical indicates liquid, right side looks like a decanter).
茶　　*tea* (*vegetation* radical indicates tea leaves + umbrella shape for drinking tea under).
薬　　*medicine* (*vegetation* and *tree* indicate herbal medicine. 白 (*white*) + four short strokes = aspirin dissolving!).
洗　　*wash* (*water* radical on left).

Now you are going to match some common signs and shop names with their English equivalents.

a	bookshop (two answers)	1	公園　　( )
b	a newsstand, a kiosk	2	薬局　　( )
c	pharmacy (two answers)	3	市場　　( )
d	butcher's	4	図書館　( )
e	toilet (hand washing)	5	酒屋　　( )
f	art gallery	6	喫茶店　( )
g	greengrocer's (800 varieties!)		(focus on 2nd + 3rd 漢字)
h	park	7	売店　　( )
i	fishmonger's	8	薬屋　　( )
j	market (place)	9	書店　　( )
k	library	10	肉屋　　( )
l	tea/coffee shop	11	飲酒店　( )
m	wine shop, liquor store	12	美術館　( )
n	drinking place, bar	13	工場　　( )
o	factory	14	八百屋　( )
		15	本屋　　( )
		16	魚屋　　( )
		17	お手洗い　　( )

Explanation: More about places

How did you get on with this activity? Some of the words need further explanation. 八百屋 (*greengrocer's*) literally means '800 shop' so think of 800 types of fruit and vegetables! You should have worked out the meaning of 喫茶店 (*coffee/tea shop*) from the second and third 漢字. The first one 喫 has a general meaning of 'eat, drink, smoke' and its radical 口 (*mouth*) indicates this general meaning. It is not widely used and focusing on the second two 漢字 gives you the meaning. 工場 (*factory*) and 市場 (*market*) are both places which have grounds and so use 場 for *place*.

Finally, お手洗い (*toilet*) has hiragana お (*o*) at the beginning which is used in front of some words to make them sound more polite and genteel. This is sometimes translated as 'honourable', so in this case 'the honourable hand washing (place)' although its real meaning is toilet! The end hiragana い is sometimes left off.

Kanji build up: More place names

As explained in the introduction, these sections will teach additional 漢字 words which you can leave out or come back to later if you feel you have taken in enough at this stage.

The following 漢字 are key to the additional place names introduced further on:

1 主 (*master*)   2 駅 (*station*)
3 便 (*convenience; mail*)   4 行 (*go*)

Now let's look at them in detail.

1 主 looks like a candlestick with a flame on top so you can remember it as 'candle' (its real meaning is *master*). It is a component of the following two 漢字:

駐 (*reside, stop-over*)   住 (*reside, dwell*)

駐 The radical is 馬 (*horse*). In old times, stop-over places or inns were a place to rest horses on a long journey. A welcoming candle in the window would light your way.

住 The radical is 人 (*person*). A person is master (real meaning of 主) in their own residence.

> **Places**
> 駐車場 *car park* (stop-over place for vehicles)
> 住所 *address* (place of residence)

2 駅 The radical is *horse*, the right side 尺 is the measurement *foot*. Think of it in this case as being 'R' for 'railway'. *Meaning: railway station* (before trains, transport was by horse!).

3 便 (*convenience; mail*) The left side is *person*, the right is 一 (*one*) and 曳 (*tug*). Here are two words it is used in – you supply the story!

> **Places**
> 便所 *toilet, urinal* (A place for your convenience, perhaps? The first 漢字 might conjure up a strong image here!)
> 郵便局 *post office* (first two 漢字 both mean *mail* plus 局 – *bureau*)

4 行 (*to go*) The radical 彳 means *going person*.

> **Places**
> 銀行 (*bank*) 銀 means *silver* (radical 金 is *metal*). **Story:** go to the bank to get silver (money).
> 商店街 (*shopping area*) You should recognize 店 (shop), 商 means *trade*, 街 consists of 'double earth' (土) between 行 and means *street* or *quarters* (earth piled up to make a road).
> 旅行案内所 (*travel information*) 旅行 means *travel*. 旅 has the left-side radical 方 which means *direction*, the right side comes from 衣 meaning *clothes*. **Story:** go (行) in the direction of a holiday with a suitcase of clothes! 案内所 means *information (place)*. Quick story for 案: tourists would certainly want more **information** about a woman wearing a large hat in a tree! (内 is introduced later in this unit).

5 More places containing 所 (*place*):

両替所 (*money exchange place*). 両 means *both*. You can see 山 (*mountain*) within this with a small mountain on **both** sides of the large one! The upper part of 替 (*exchange*) looks like two people who are **exchanging**. **Both** gain from the exchange!

精算所 (*fare adjustment office*). You learnt the first 漢字 in Unit 7: it means *purity* or *white rice*. The radical means *rice*. Focus on this meaning to give you a story for the whole word. In ancient times, rice rather than money was used as payment including fares!

And did you know, if you travel by underground in Japan and do not know the fare to your destination, buy the cheapest ticket and pay the difference when you arrive, at the 精算所 – *fare adjustment office*.

6 More places containing 場 (*place*):

切符売場 (*ticket office*). 売場 literally means 'selling place'. 切 means *cut* (刀 means *sword*). 符 means *token* and has 竹 (*bamboo*) at the top and 付 (*attach*) below. Maybe in ancient times a ticket was a token cut from bamboo!

劇場 (*theatre*). 劇 means *drama*. If you look hard enough you can make out the outline of the arch and curtains around a stage with a kabuki actor standing in the middle!

7 More places containing 館 (*hall*):

映画館 (*cinema*). Focus on 画 which means *picture* but you can also see within it four squares representing the screens of a multi-screen cinema!

旅館 (*Japanese inn*). 旅 means *travel*. A place to stay when travelling.

博物館 (*museum*). You learnt 物 in Unit 4 – it means *things*. Focus on 博 meaning *PhD* or *esteem*. Esteemed items are kept in museums. Also, think of the left side of 博 as an ancient Japanese sword!

練習二　Activity 2

In the previous kanji build up section you were introduced to 15 more place names. The following activity gives you the chance to see how many you can now recognize. If you do not get them all on the first try, simply go back over the explanations – then try again!

Match the English words (there are clues in brackets) to the 漢字 words in the box.

a   travel information (*woman in tree*)
b   Japanese inn (*travel place*)
c   museum (*Japanese sword*)
d   theatre (*proscenium arch*)
e   car park (*stop-overs for horses!*)
f   address (*master of residence*)
g   fare adjustment office (*pay with rice*)
h   money exchange (*two people exchange*)
i   shopping area (*double earth for road*)
j   railway station (*horse + R for railway*)
k   ticket office (*cut bamboo selling place!*)
l   bank (*go to bank for silver money*)
m   cinema (*four squares = four screens*)
n   post office (*mail bureau*)
o   toilet (*convenience / your own story*)

1 駐車場 ( )	2 住所 ( )	3 駅 ( )
4 便所 ( )	5 郵便局 ( )	6 銀行 ( )
7 商店街 ( )	8 旅行案内所 ( )	9 両替所 ( )
10 精算所 ( )	11 切符売場 ( )	12 劇場 ( )
13 映画館 ( )	14 旅館 ( )	15 博物館 ( )

Explanation: Kanji signs

You have so far been exposed to a total of 47 place names (or 32 if you missed out the kanji build up section). Next you are going to learn to recognize more common signs and written information containing 漢字 or components that you are already familiar with. These are:

1   車 (*vehicle*)   2   室 (*room*)   3   国 (*country*)
4   席 (*seat*)   5   物 (*thing*)   6   料 (*fee*)

Now let us look at these in detail.

1   車 (*vehicle*). Here are five 漢字 words containing 車:

空車 *unoccupied taxi*   満車 *occupied taxi*
列車 *long-distance train*   寝台車 *sleeper train*
自転車 *bicycle*

空車 and 満車. These signs are displayed on the windscreens of taxi cabs and at car parks. 空 means *sky* or *empty* and, if you look carefully, looks like an aeroplane taking off into the air from a runway! It is also used in 空港 (*airport*).

満 means *full* or *enough*. The radical is *water* and it contains a component you have already learnt in this unit, 両 (*both*). Above this is the component *vegetation*. **Story**: water and vegetation together are **enough** to live on!

列車. You have already learnt 電車 (*electric train*). This is used generically but also for local trains, whereas 列車 denotes long-distance trains. The right-hand component 刂 looks like a long rail track!

寝台車. 台 means *pedestal* but can you see a person with a large nose ム lying on a bed! 寝 means *to sleep* and has the radical 宀 (*lid*), in this case *roof*. On the left is a component which looks like a bed standing upright – the type you pull down from the wall on a train.

自転車. You met 転 (*turn, rotate*) in Unit 7. 自 means *automatic* or *self*. You can see 目 (*eye*) with an extra short stroke. Think of this as a small nose (between the eyes!). The Japanese point to their nose (rather than their chest) when they refer to 'me'. Altogether we have 'self-rotating vehicle', in other words, a *bicycle*!

2 室 (*room*). This is similar to 屋 (*store*) which you learnt earlier in this unit (on p. 106). The radical is different. Here it is 宀 (*lid, roof*). The lower part is 至 (*arrive*) but focus on its difference from *shop* because it has a roof – 'rooms have roofs'. Here are two 漢字 words containing 室:

洋室 *Western-style room*   和室 *Japanese-style room*

洋室 and 和室 are words used in hotels and estate agents. 和室 (*Japanese-style rooms*) have tatami mats on the floor, futon mattresses to sleep on and Japanese baths whereas 洋室 (*Western-style rooms*) have carpets on the floor and in hotels have Western beds and bathrooms.

洋 means *ocean* (the West is across the ocean!) and the radical is *water*. The right side 羊 means *sheep* (can you see the horns of the ram?), an animal associated with the West.

和 is the old Chinese word for Japan. You learnt it as *peace* in Unit 3 (as part of the *Shōwa* era). The left side 禾 represents the ears of rice as it grows in the fields, and rice is Japan's staple food.

3 国 (*country*). Here are five words containing this 漢字:

國内 *domestic*   外國 *abroad, foreign*
外國為替 *foreign exchange*   國際電話 *international phone*
入國管理 *passport control*

内 means *inside* (inside the country). You can see a person 人 inside a frame. (Do not confuse with 肉 *flesh* – two persons in a frame).

外 means *outside* (outside the country). The radical 夕 means *evening* (imagine it as a crescent moon shape) and imagine a person 卜 standing outside looking at the moon. 外国人 means *foreigner* (outsider). 外国為替 contains 替 meaning *exchange* (p. 109).

国際電話. You learnt 電話 (*telephone*) in Unit 6. 際 is used to indicate *international* and consists of the radical *village* (think of the global village) and 祭 meaning *festival*. (Think of the upper part being a marquee and the lower part a trestle table, set up for a fête or **festival**.)

入国管理. First you have *enter the country* (to enter a country you have to show your passport). Focus then on 管. You learnt on p. 106 that the component 官 means *government* and passport control is a government or civil service organization.

4 席 (*seat*). The radical is 广 (*dotted cliff*) but for this 漢字 imagine it is the roof and side of a train carriage (with electric cable on the roof). The component within looks like a computer game character! He has a square head, stick body and arms. You cannot see his legs because he is sitting down! Here are two signs containing 席:

自由席 *unreserved seat* **指定席** *reserved seat*

You have already learnt that 自 means *self*. 自由 means *freedom* – the freedom to make your own (self) decisions. With 席 it means *free / unreserved seat*.

指 means *finger / indicate*. The general meaning is indicated by the left-hand radical *hand* (from 手). 定 means *fixed*. The general meaning (putting a limit on something) is indicated by the radical 宀 (a crown or in this case a *lid*). Therefore the seats indicated are limited/reserved.

Note: 定食 means *set meal* (in other words, the menu is **fixed**).

5 物 (*thing*). You first learnt this in Unit 4 (p. 51).

荷物 *luggage, parcel*
忘れ物 *left behind by mistake / lost luggage*

Look at 荷 as a picture of a suitcase (口) coming through the conveyor belt at the airport! 忘 means *forgotten*. Remember that the radical 心 (*heart*) is used for emotions and thoughts. 亡 means *deceased* or *lost*.

6 料 (*fee*). Focus on the radical 米 (*rice*) which you know can represent payment:

料金   means *fee* (*lit.* 'fee money')
入場料   means *entrance fee* (*lit.* 'enter place fee')
無料   means *admission free* (*lit.* 'no fee'). 無 means *nothing* and looks like a prison window with **no** prisoner inside!

練習三   Activity 3

In the last section you were introduced to 22 new information words and three new general 漢字 (室、席、料). Test yourself by seeing how many you can recognize (write the English meanings in the brackets). If you cannot remember all of them at first, check your answers by looking back through the section.

空車 ( )   満車 ( )   列車 ( )   寝台車 ( )
自転車 ( )   洋室 ( )   和室 ( )   国内 ( )
外国 ( )   外国人 ( )   外国為替 ( )
国際電話 ( )   入国管理 ( )   祭 ( )
自由席 ( )   指定席 ( )   定食 ( )   荷物 ( )
忘れ物 ( )   料金 ( )   入場料 ( )   無料 ( )

Kanji build up: More signs

As with the last kanji build up section, you can leave this one out and come back to it later if you wish to.

1 Here are three compound words containing 室 (*room*):

浴室 *bathroom*   化粧室 *powder room, toilet*
待合室 *waiting room*

浴室. 浴 means *bathe* and has the *water* radical on the left. The right-hand component looks like a house, as in 'bath house'!

Note: The word for a *Japanese-style bath* is 風呂. This type of bath is deeper and shorter than Western baths, and you sit with your knees bent and only your head above water. 呂 means *backbone* (can you see the vertebrae?) – you sit in the bath with back straight.

化粧室. 化粧 means *cosmetics* (think of the *rice* radical 米 as a powder puff!). Powder room is a euphemism for ladies' toilet or bathroom.

待合室. Focus on 待 which means *wait*. The left-hand radical is *going person* and the right-hand radical is 寺 (*temple*).

2   In the previous section (p. 112) you learnt 和 (*Japanese*) and 洋 (*Western*). Here are four more words containing these:

和食 *Japanese cuisine*   **洋食** *Western cuisine*
和式 *Japanese-style*   **洋式** *Western-style*

練習四   Activity 4

In the last section you were introduced to eight new compound words. Can you match them up with their English meanings?

1   和食   a   Western-style
2   和式   b   Japanese-style
3   待合室   c   Western cuisine
4   浴室   d   Japanese cuisine
5   風呂   e   bathroom
6   化粧室   f   (Japanese) bath
7   洋食   g   waiting room
8   洋式   h   powder room (ladies' toilet)

Explanation: A map of Japan

In this section you will learn to recognize the main islands and cities of Japan. First, you are going to learn the four compass directions:

And here are quick clues to help you remember them:

北   *north* (looks like two people sitting back to back to keep warm (cold in the North))
南   *south* (yen symbol ¥ (more money in the South of Japan!))
東   *east* (components: *sun* and *tree*. Sun rising in the East from behind the tree)
西   *west* (looks like 四 *four* – do not confuse them – and it is the fourth compass direction)

Now look at the map of Japan (overleaf) with the main islands and cities labelled in 漢字 and *rōmaji*. How many 漢字 do you recognize? There is a list of clues on the next page to help you learn the names. You have not learnt any of the 漢字 for 3, 6 and 12. They are included for interest only.

① NIHON (Japan)
日本

HOKKAIDŌ ②
北海道
Sapporo ③
札幌

Hiroshima
広島

京都
Kyōto

大阪
Osaka

Nagasaki
長崎 ⑫

④ HONSHŪ 本州

Tōkyō 東京 ⑤

⑥

⑦

⑩ SHIKOKU 四国

⑪ KYŪSHŪ 九州

Yokohama 横浜

	Place	漢字 Meanings	Story clue
1	日本	*sun, root*	'Land of the rising sun'
2	北海道	*North, sea, way*	'North island across the sea'
3	札幌	*paper money, hood*	Winter Olympics held here – brought in money!
4	本州	*root/main, province*	Main (biggest) island of Japan
5	東京	*East, capital*	(Which it is!)
6	横浜	*side, seacoast*	'City on the seacoast to the side of Tokyo'
7	大阪	*big, slope*	Osaka is built on a hillside
8	京都	*capital, city*	Kyoto used to be the capital of Japan
9	広島	*wide, island*	Hiroshima stands in a wide bay dotted with small islands
10	四国	*four, country*	Shikoku is the fourth of the main islands of Japan
11	九州	*nine, province*	Kyushu is divided into nine provinces (administrative)
12	長崎	*long, promontory*	Describes Nagasaki harbour

Explanation: Warning signs

It is very useful and often essential to be able to read this type of sign. A friend of mine drove up a closed road and got stuck in a snow drift because she could not read the sign at the head of the road. After that she learnt to recognize 禁 (*forbidden*) as 'two Harry Worths (the entertainer who used to stand half behind mirrors lifting his leg and arm up and down) dancing on a picnic table'! That 漢字 alone would have prevented her going up that road.

We start by learning some general warning 漢字 then look at how they are used.

禁 *forbidden* (just mentioned)
禁止 *no, not allowed* (止 means *stop*)
嚴禁 *strictly forbidden*　煙 *to smoke* (*fire* radical)
中 *middle*. In signs means *during* or *under*

練習五　Activity 5

Here are some common warning signs using the 漢字 we have just met plus ones you know already.

Match each word to its English meaning.

1　駐車禁止　　　a　Outdoor shoes strictly forbidden (　)
2　立入禁止　　　b　No smoking (　)
3　禁煙　　　　　c　No parking (　)
4　土足嚴禁　　　d　Under construction (　)
5　工事中　　　　e　No admittance (　)

Finally in this section, three more useful warning signs with clues to remember:

非常口 *Emergency exit* (非 looks like a path cleared of clutter for easy access)
注意 *Caution* (注 *Story*: 'pour water on a candle to caution against fire'!)
危險 *Danger* (危 looks like a snake in a box – dangerous if it escapes!)

Explanation: Pairs of signs

This is the final Explanation section! Ten 漢字 follow which can be paired as opposites in meaning.

左 *left*	Use of 工 for **I** (am / am not left handed)
右 *right*	口 ('Tick the **right** box')
押す *push*	Hand radical is **push**ing the doorbell
引く *pull*	引 looks like an archery bow which you **pull**
開 *open*	Gates (elevator doors). Two people holding one door each **open**
閉 *close*	One person cannot hold the doors and they **close**
到着 *arrival*	Remember that 至 means *arrive* or 'the nose of the plane touching ground'
出発 *departure*	出 means *go out*
営業中 *open for business*	営 is a backbone with a hat on – a shop assistant!
休業中 *closed*	休 means *holiday*

Kanji build up: Miscellaneous signs

And finally, some miscellaneous signs. Once more, you can miss this section out if you need to consolidate what you have learnt so far.

焼 means *grilled* (*fire* radical plus component looking like a barbecue). Look at these words:

焼肉	*yakiniku* – grilled meat
焼き鳥	*yakitori* – barbecued chicken on bamboo skewers
お好み焼き	*okonomiyaki* – a type of thick pancake cooked on an iron griddle at your table
すき焼き	*sukiyaki* – beef grilled then cooked with vegetables in a cast iron pot
新幹線	*shinkansen* or bullet train. 新 (new) helps you to remember this
地下鉄	*underground* (train). *Lit*: 'ground under iron'. Iron indicates the rail track
急行	*express* (train). *Lit*: 'hurry go'
特急	*special express. Lit*: 'special hurry'

Look at the pictures of various Japanese signs. There is a range of written styles, both vertical and horizontal left to right. How many can you recognize? You may need to come back to this activity after you have worked through the conclusion (which includes a review of all the signs learnt in this unit) but keep a score and see if you can improve on it!

1

2

3

4

The name of a temple entrance

5

6

7

8

9

10

11

下北沢駅

SHIMOKITAZAWA

What is Shimokitazawa the name of? (Focus on the last kanji)

12

The first two kanji mean *Fuji*. What is this building called?

13 営業時間

14 国際電話

15 自由

16 空車

17 和室

18 立入禁止

19 禁煙

終りに　Conclusion

おめでとう (*omedetō*) Congratulations! You have worked through a minimum of 76 漢字 signs in this unit. This does not include the 12 island and city names, and the 31 signs in the kanji build up sections. This makes an overall total of 119 signs, which is a huge amount and obviously you are not going to remember them all in one go. To help you review and consolidate your learning, all the signs are grouped below by theme. How many do you remember? The English is also given at the end of the unit so test yourself, then check and use these pages as a check list. (Signs taught in the kanji build up sections are marked with an asterisk.)

ℹ️ Remembering kanji words

Try writing out the words on small squares of card. Put the 漢字 on one side and the English on the other. Use these mini flashcards to test yourself by looking at the 漢字 side, giving your answer then turning the card over to see if you are right. Try doing ten in the morning, ten in the evening and gradually build up the number you can remember.

General

1 出口	2 入口	3 女	4 男
5 大人	6 小人	7 お手洗い	8 便所*
9 化粧室	10 左	11 右	12 和式*
13 洋式*			

Shopping and places in town

1 店	2 肉屋	3 八百屋	4 本屋
5 魚屋	6 酒屋	7 喫茶店	8 飲酒店
9 書店	10 売店	11 薬局	12 薬屋
13 市場	14 公園	15 図書館	16 商店街*
17 国際電話	18 銀行*	19 郵便局*	20 外国為替
21 両替所*	22 駐車場*	23 押す	24 引く
25 開	26 閉	27 営業中	28 休業中
29 工場	30 学校		

Sightseeing and entertainment

1 美術館	2 お寺	3 休日	4 祭
5 映画館*	6 博物館*	7 劇場*	8 料金
9 入場料	10 無料		

Travel and transport

1 北	2 南	3 東
4 西	5 外国人	6 到着
7 出発	8 入国管理	9 国内
10 駅*	11 電車	12 上り
13 下り	14 列車	15 寝台車
16 自由席	17 指定席	18 荷物
19 忘れ物	20 精算所*	21 切符売場*
22 旅行案内所*	23 新幹線*	24 急行*
25 特急*	26 地下鉄*	27 空車
28 満車	29 自転車	30 待合室*

Accommodation

1 旅館*	2 洋室	3 和室
4 浴室*	5 風呂*	6 住所*

Warnings

1 駐車禁止   2 立入禁止   3 禁煙   4 土足厳禁
5 工事中   6 非常口   7 注意   8 危険

Food and drink

1 和食*   2 洋食*   3 焼肉*
4 焼き鳥*   5 お好み焼き*   6 すき焼き*

English meanings

General

1 exit
2 entrance
3 woman
4 man
5 adult
6 child
7 toilet
8 toilet
9 toilet / powder room
10 left
11 right
12 Japanese-style
13 Western-style

Shopping and places in town

1 shop
2 butcher
3 greengrocer
4 book shop
5 fish shop
6 liquor store
7 coffee shop
8 bar
9 bookstore
10 kiosk
11 and 12 pharmacy/chemist's
13 market
14 park
15 library
16 shopping area
17 international telephone
18 bank
19 post office
20 foreign exchange
21 exchange bureau
22 car park
23 push
24 pull
25 open
26 close
27 open (for business)
28 closed
29 factory
30 school

Sightseeing and entertainment

1 art gallery   2 temple   3 holiday   4 festival
5 cinema   6 museum   7 theatre   8 fee
9 entrance fee   10 admission free

Travel and transport

1 north
2 south
3 east
4 west
5 foreigner
6 arrival
7 departure
8 passport control
9 domestic
10 station

11 train
12 up
13 down
14 long-distance train
15 sleeper
16 unreserved seat
17 reserved seat
18 luggage
19 lost property
20 fare adjustment office
21 ticket office
22 travel information
23 bullet train
24 express
25 special express
26 underground/subway
27 unoccupied (taxi)
28 occupied (taxi)
29 bicycle
30 waiting room

Accommodation

1 Japanese inn
2 Western-style room
3 Japanese-style room
4 bathroom
5 (Japanese) bath
6 address

Warnings

1 no parking
2 no admittance
3 no smoking
4 outdoor shoes strictly forbidden
5 under construction
6 emergency exit
7 caution
8 danger

Food and drink

1 Japanese cuisine
2 Western cuisine
3 yakiniku – grilled meat
4 yakitori – grilled chicken
5 okonomiyaki – grilled pancake
6 sukiyaki – beef 'hot pot'

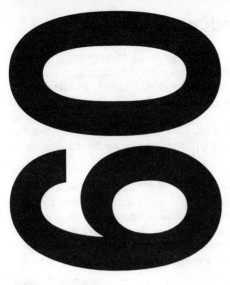

09

unit 9 第九課 unit 9

In this unit you will
- learn to read the 46 **カタカナ** (*katakana*) symbols which make up the phonetic 'alphabet'
- learn some rules for making extra sounds from the 46 main symbols
- be introduced to picture–sound associations to make learning easier
- learn how to write **カタカナ** (*katakana*)
- have a go at reading some words and phrases

はじめに Introduction

カタカナ (*katakana*) is the script used to represent foreign words which have been adopted into the Japanese language (loanwords) and foreign names (personal names, countries etc.). Most of the loanwords are derived from English words and this means that once you can read the script you can normally work out what a word means. This makes カタカナ a fun script to learn and working out the meanings can be an enjoyable challenge!

In Unit 5 you learnt to read the ひらがな script. You may have decided to work through the 漢字 units first and then to work on Units 5 and 9. And you could work through this unit without learning ひらがな first but as most of the rules are the same for both scripts you will be referred back to the appropriate page in Unit 5 to read through the explanations there.

Begin by looking back to the section of the introduction which deals with an overview of the different types of Japanese script (pp. viii–x) and the section on カタカナ. Can you answer these questions based on the information you have just read?

1 What is カタカナ used for? (name four uses)
2 What do カタカナ symbols originate from?
3 How many basic symbols make up the カタカナ syllabary?

Work it out!

You have not learnt to read any カタカナ yet (apart from these three symbols) but as you did in Unit 5 you are going to pair up カタカナ words which are the same. There are six words (a–f) in the left column which are repeated in a different order in the right column. Match up the same words and write the correct letter in the brackets on the left. The first one is done for you.

a	ケーキ	スカート	( )
b	アイス	ステーキ	( )
c	トースト	ケーキ	(a)
d	ステーキ	スーツ	( )
e	スカート	アイス	( )
f	スーツ	トースト	( )

Explanation: How to read katakana

Let us begin by looking at the first four lines of the カタカナ syllabary with the romanized pronunciation and learn how to read them. The order and pronunciation is exactly the same as ひらがな (see pp. 60–1 to refresh your memory). Only the symbols are different. The chart is written in the traditional way from top to bottom right to left. This is to give you practice at reading vertically. Remember that you read in columns not rows and begin to read from the top right symbol.

ta タ	sa サ	ka カ	a ア
chi チ	shi シ	ki キ	i イ
tsu ツ	su ス	ku ク	u ウ
te テ	se セ	ke ケ	e エ
to ト	so ソ	ko コ	o オ

練習一　Activity 1

In the Work it out! activity you matched six カタカナ words. Now you are going to try to read those words. Use the chart of the first 20 symbols and say the words out loud then see if you can match them to their English meanings in the box that follows. Remember that カタカナ is used to write foreign (mainly English) words. The pronunciation is adapted to suit Japanese pronunciation rules (every consonant is followed by a vowel) but you can usually recognize the word once you have read it correctly. A dash ー after a symbol means that you lengthen the sound of that symbol (う [u] performs this function in ひらがな. See p. 67).

a ケーキ　　**b** トースト　　**c** ステーキ
d アイス　　**e** スカート　　**f** スーツ

skirt ( )	suit ( )	steak ( )
cake ( )	ice ( )	toast ( )

❶ Remembering katakana

In Unit 5 you were introduced to the idea of remembering ひらがな through visual and sound association (p. 64). Here are a few ideas for カタカナ symbols to get you started. Try to think of your own and write them down. Some symbols are easier than others but just do a few at a time.

ア **(a)** looks like an antelope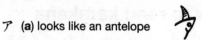

イ **(i)** is a leaning **T** which rhymes with **i**

ウ **(u)** looks like a **uisukii** (*whisky*) flask

エ **(e)** looks like elevator doors

キ **(ki)** looks like a door key

Explanation: The katakana chart

You are now going to be introduced to the whole カタカナ chart, including the correct order in which to write each symbol. This follows exactly the same format as for ひらがな in Unit 5 (p. 61).

ナ na	タ ta	サ sa	カ ka	ア a
ナ	タ	サ	カ	ア
一ナ	ノクタ	一ヤサ	フカ	フア
二 ni	チ chi	シ shi	キ ki	イ i
二	チ	シ	キ	イ
一二	ノ一チ	丶シ	一ニキ	ノイ
ヌ nu	ツ tsu	ス su	ク ku	ウ u
ヌ	ツ	ス	ク	ウ
フヌ	丶丶ツ	フス	ノク	丶ウ
ネ ne	テ te	セ se	ケ ke	エ e
ネ	テ	セ	ケ	エ
丶ラネネ	一ニテ	フセ	ノトケ	一丁エ
ノ no	ト to	ソ so	コ ko	オ o
ノ	ト	ソ	コ	オ
ノ	丨ト	丶ソ	フコ	一ナオ

As with ひらがな try to learn to write カタカナ because this will help you to remember how to read them too. Look carefully at the stroke order and remember that in general you write horizontal strokes from left to right and vertical/diagonal strokes from top to bottom (variations to the direction are marked with an arrow on the individual symbol).

ℹ️ Organize your learning

Don't worry about learning all the symbols in one go – keep referring back to the charts.

You might find it useful to make a カタカナ vocabulary book for this unit. You could either organize the words by theme (food, drink, clothes, electrical gadgets etc.) or alphabetically using the 46 basic symbols (one per page) and enter all words beginning with a

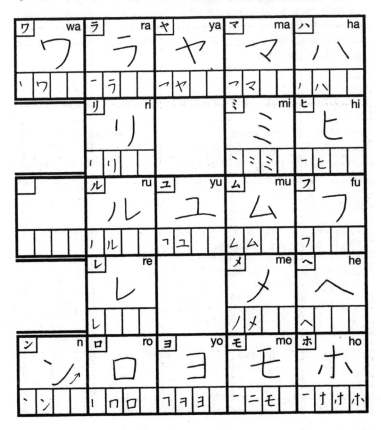

particular symbol on the same page. Whichever way you choose, write out each カタカナ word with its *rōmaji* pronunciation (optional) and its English meaning next to it. You can then test yourself by covering up the English and seeing if you can read the カタカナ word. And it will form a useful dictionary too!

練習二 Activity 2

Now that you have been introduced to the 46 カタカナ symbols, it is time to put your learning into practice and have a go at reading some words. As in Unit 5, the words are in three sets. Set 1 refers to the first part of the chart, set 2 refers to the second and set 3 to the whole chart. You also have to select the correct English meanings so say the words out loud. You may be able to do this even if you cannot read all the かな (*kana*) symbols. See how many symbols/words you can read from memory before using the chart to search for those you cannot remember. Keep coming back to this activity and try to improve your score each time!

Explanation: Pronunciation of *r* and *l*

Japanese pronunciation does not distinguish between *r* and *l* sounds. Try replacing *r* sounds with *l* sounds if you cannot work out the meaning. For example ランチ (*ranchi*) means *lunch*.

Set 1

a ケーキ b ココア c タクシー d コート
e セーター f スキー g スケート

1 skating ( )   2 skiing ( )   3 cocoa ( )
4 taxi ( )   5 cake ( )   6 sweater ( )
7 coat ( )

Set 2

a ラーメン b ハム c メモ
d メロン e レモン

1 memo ( )   2 lemon ( )   3 melon ( )
4 ham ( )   5 *rāmen* (Chinese noodles) ( )

Set 3

a チキン	b アイスクリーム	c カレー
d ライス	e トマト	f レストラン
g テニス	h カメラ	

1 restaurant ( )	**2** tennis ( )	**3** rice ( )
4 chicken ( )	**5** curry ( )	**6** ice cream ( )
7 camera ( )	**8** tomato ( )	

ℹ Similar katakana

You have probably already confused some of the similar-looking カタカナ. This section will line these up so that you can look at the differences and keep them separate in your mind.

ア、マ (a, ma)　　　　サ、セ (sa, se)

ク、タ、ヌ (ku, ta, nu)　　ウ、フ、ワ (u, fu, wa)

ナ、メ (na, me)　　　　ル、レ (ru, re)

シ、ツ (shi, tsu)　　　* The long stroke in シ is written upwards (like a tick) and the short strokes are almost at right angles to the long stroke.

The long stroke in ツ is written downwards and is at a steeper angle. The short strokes stand side by side.

ン、ソ (n, so)　　　　* ン has the same features as シ and ソ has the same features as ツ (but each only has one short stroke).

ℹ Similar hiragana and katakana

The good news is that some カタカナ symbols are very similar to their ひらがな equivalents (in many cases they originated from the same 漢字). This can make them easier to remember. They are listed here, ひらがな first then カタカナ:

う、ウ (u)	か、カ (ka)	き、キ (ki)
け、ケ (ke)	こ、コ (ko)	せ、セ (se)
に、ニ (ni)	へ、ヘ (he)	も、モ (mo)
や、ヤ (ya)	り、リ (ri)	

Explanation: Katakana that change their sound

Again, the rules are exactly the same as for ひらがな, only the script is different. Read over the ひらがな section again (p. 68) then fill in the gaps in the following activity. And remember, just as with all the units in this book, **you** set the pace!

練習三　Activity 3

When you add ˚ (*ten ten*) to certain symbols you get a change in sound.

1　*k* sounds become *g* sounds (hard *g* as in *get*):

カ、キ、ク、ケ、コ　→　ガ、ギ、グ、ゲ、ゴ
(*ka*) (*ki*) (*ku*) (*ke*) (*ko*)　（　）（　）（　）（　）（　）

2　*s* sounds → *z* sounds:

サ、シ、ス、セ、ソ　→　ザ、ジ、ズ、ゼ、ゾ
(*sa*) (*shi*) (*su*) (*se*) (*so*)　（　）（　）*（　）（　）（　）

3　*t* sounds become *d* sounds:

タ、テ、ト　→　ダ、デ、ド
(*ta*) (*te*) (*to*)　（　）（　）（　）

4　*h* sounds become *b* sounds:

ハ、ヒ、フ、ヘ、ホ　→　バ、ビ、ブ、ベ、ボ
(*ha*) (*hi*) (*fu*) (*he*) (*ho*)　（　）（　）（　）（　）（　）

5　In addition, *h* sounds become *p* sounds when a small circle ˚ is added:

ハ、ヒ、フ、ヘ、ホ　→　パ、ピ、プ、ペ、ポ
(*ha*) (*hi*) (*fu*) (*he*) (*ho*)　（　）（　）（　）（　）（　）

Check whether you have filled in the brackets correctly by referring back to this section in Unit 5 (pp. 68–9).

練習四　Activity 4

This activity is designed to help you build up your confidence in reading カタカナ and to ease you away from referring back to the charts (but they are always there if you need them!). This will be done by re-introducing a few カタカナ symbols at a time and getting you to read words which contain them. Section by section you will build up the number of symbols until you are reading words containing them all. For each section look over the カタカナ symbols then match up the words and meanings beneath them. When a symbol has linked sounds (for example, カ(*ka*)、ガ(*ga*)) they are given together but not all are necessarily used in that section.

1

> サ (sa)、ザ (za)、シ (shi)、ジ (ji)、ス (su)、ズ (zu)、
> チ (chi)、テ (te)、デ (de)、ト (to)、ド (do)、ン (n)

a トースト　　b デザート　　c チーズ
d ジーンズ　　e シーン

i jeans ( )　　　　　ii cheese ( )　　iii toast ( )
iv (movie) scene ( )　　v dessert ( )

2

> カ (ka)、ガ (ga)、セ (se)、ゼ (ze)、ソ (so)、ゾ (zo)、
> ツ (tsu)、ハ (ha)、バ (ba)、パ (pa)

a ソーセージ　　b ハンバーガー　　c パンツ
d バス　　　　　e スカート

i pants, trousers ( )　　ii skirt ( )
iii sausage ( )　　　　　iv bus or bath ( )
v hamburger ( )

3

> コ (ko)、ゴ (go)、タ (ta)、ダ (da)、ヒ (hi)、ビ (bi)、
> ピ (pi)、フ (fu)、ブ (bu)、プ (pu)

a スカーフ　　b テープ　　c ピザ　　　d パブ
e ヒーター　　f タバコ　　g ダンス

i tobacco (cigarettes) ( )　　ii (cassette) tape ( )
iii heater ( )　　　　　　　　iv pub ( )
v scarf ( )　　　　　　　　　vi pizza ( )
vii dance ( )

4

> キ (ki)、ギ (gi)、ケ (ke)、ゲ (ge)、ヘ (he)、ベ (be)、
> ペ (pe)、ホ (ho)、ボ (bo)、ポ (po)

a チキン　　b ギター　　　c パスポート
d ペン　　　e スーツケース　f ボタン
g ベンチ

i passport ( )　　ii suitcase ( )　　iii chicken ( )
iv pen ( )　　　　v bench ( )　　　　vi guitar ( )
vii button ( )

5

> ラ (*ra*)、リ (*ri*)、ル* (*ru*)、レ (*re*)、ロ (*ro*) (*l* or *r* sound can be used for these)

* ル is often used as the final *l* sound, for example, ホテル (*hotel*)、プール (*pool*).

a サラダ	b カレー	c レンタカー
d レストラン	e フロント	f アイスリンク
g テーブル	h ダブル	i ゴルフ
j ビール	k セール	l ベースボール

  i table ( )   ii curry ( )
 iii golf ( )   iv front (reception) ( )
  v beer ( )   vi salad ( )
 vii sale ( )   viii double ( )
 ix ice rink ( )   x baseball ( )
 xi rental car ( )   xii restaurant ( )

6

> ク (*ku*)、グ (*gu*)、マ (*ma*)、ミ (*mi*)、ム (*mu*)、メ (*me*)、
> モ (*mo*)

a トマト	b ミルク	c ハム
d カメラ	e グラム	f モカ

  i tomato ( )   ii ham ( )   iii gram ( )
 iv camera ( )   v mocha (coffee) ( )   vi milk ( )

7

> ナ (*na*)、ニ (*ni*)、ヌ (*nu*)、ネ (*ne*)、ノ (*no*)

a バナナ	b テニス	c ネクタイ
d ノート	e カヌー	

  i tennis ( )   ii canoe ( )   iii banana ( )
 iv necktie ( )   v note(book) ( )

8

> ア (*a*)、イ (*i*)、ウ (*u*)、エ (*e*)、オ (*o*)、ワ (*wa*)

a アイスクリーム	b ブラウス	c エスカレーター
d ステレオ	e ワイン	

  i ice cream ( )   ii escalator ( )   iii wine ( )
 iv stereo ( )   v blouse ( )

Explanation: Contracted sounds

The only three symbols you did not use in the last activity were ヤ、ユ、ヨ (*ya, yu, yo*). These are used as normal symbols but also are used to form contracted sounds. You learnt about these for ひらがな in Unit 5. The rules are the same for カタカナ. Read back over this section (p. 67) to remind or familiarize yourself with the rules before trying the next activity.

練習五　Activity 5

Write the pronunciation of the contracted カタカナ sounds in the brackets. The first line has been done for you:

キ (*ki*) → キャ (*kya*)	キュ (*kyu*)	キョ (*kyo*)
ギ (*gi*) → ギャ ( )	ギュ ( )	ギョ ( )
シ (*shi*) → シャ ( )	シュ ( )	ショ ( )
ジ (*ji*) → ジャ ( )	ジュ ( )	ジョ ( )
チ (*chi*) → チャ ( )	チュ ( )	チョ ( )
ニ (*ni*) → ニャ ( )	ニュ ( )	ニョ ( )
ヒ (*hi*) → ヒャ ( )	ヒュ ( )	ヒョ ( )
ビ (*bi*) → ビャ ( )	ビュ ( )	ビョ ( )
ピ (*pi*) → ピャ ( )	ピュ ( )	ピョ ( )
ミ (*mi*) → ミャ ( )	ミュ ( )	ミョ ( )
リ (*ri*) → リャ ( )	リュ ( )	リョ ( )

Now check your answers with the equivalent charts in Unit 5 (pp. 67 and 69).

練習六　Activity 6

Now let us put into practice what you have learnt above. Match the カタカナ words in the left column to their English meanings on the right.

a	キャンプ	1	computer ( )
b	シャワー	2	communication ( )
c	ジャム	3	camp(ing) ( )
d	ジュース	4	jam ( )
e	ジョギング	5	musical ( )
f	チョコレート	6	menu ( )
g	メニュー	7	shower ( )
h	コンピュータ	8	jogging ( )
i	ミュージカル	9	chocolate ( )
j	コミュニケーション	10	juice ( )

Explanation: The small ツ (*tsu*)

This was introduced for ひらがな in Unit 5 (p. 69). When you see a small ツ (*tsu*) in a word, you do not pronounce it but pause slightly (a glottal stop) before saying the next sound. In カタカナ words this has the effect of 'holding back' the next sound so that it becomes closer in pronunciation to the original word or at least easier for the Japanese to pronounce. An example will make this clearer:

ホットドッグ (*hotdog*) is pronounced *hot(to)dog(gu)*

The pronunciation of *to* and *gu* is 'held back' (and written here in brackets).

練習七 Activity 7

Match the カタカナ words with their English meanings:

a	カップ	1	toilet paper ( )
b	サンドイッチ	2	coin locker ( )
c	ミックス	3	jacket ( )
d	サッカー	4	cup ( )
e	ホッケー	5	hockey ( )
f	マッチ	6	soccer (football) ( )
g	コインロッカー	7	sandwich ( )
h	バスケットボール	8	mix ( )
i	トイレットペーパー	9	match ( )
j	ジャケット	10	basketball ( )

Explanation: Extra katakana sounds

You learnt in the introduction that there are a number of uses of カタカナ but this unit focuses on the two main uses of カタカナ: 1 to represent foreign words adopted into the Japanese language (loanwords) and 2 to represent foreign names (cities, countries, personal names, designer and brand names). However, not every sound in a foreign language has an equivalent sound in Japanese and, as you will have noticed already, this leads to changes in pronunciation when the word is adapted to Japanese. Some of these changes have already been pointed out. This section deals with the rest.

1 *th* sound. This sound does not exist in Japanese and so is replaced by *s* sounds:

マラソン *ma ra so n* (*marathon*)
サッチャー *sa t chā* (*Thatcher*)
スミス *su mi su* (*Smith*)
マシュー *ma shū* (*Matthew*)

si also does not exist and is replaced with シ (*shi*) or ジ (*ji*):

シドニー *shi do nī* (*Sydney*)
ビジネス *bi ji ne su* (*business*)

2 *er* sound. This is replaced by a lengthened *a* sound (using ー):

ハンバーガー *ha n bā gā* (*hamburger*)
ピーター *pī tā* (*Peter*)

3 Some *f* sounds are replaced with *h* sounds:

テレホンカード *te re ho n kā do* (*telephone card*)
コーヒー *kō hī* (*coffee*)

4 *v* sound. This sound does not exist naturally in Japanese, the nearest equivalent being a *b* sound:

エレベーター *e re bē tā* (*elevator*)
バレーボール *ba rē bō ru* (*volleyball*)
ビデオ *bi de o* (*video*)
ラブホテル *ra bu ho te ru* (*Love Hotel*)

There also exists a group of sounds which have been designed to represent *v* sounds:

ヴァ (*va*)   ヴィ (*vi*)   ヴ (*vu*)   ヴェ (*ve*)   ヴォ (*vo*)

The rule is that these are used in foreign names and countries but rules are often broken! Foreign names and countries are also written using the *b* sounds; other loanwords are sometimes written using the *v* sounds:

ヴィクトリア *vi ku to ri a* (*Victoria*)   or
                                  ビクトリア *bi ku to ri a*
ヴァイオリン *va i o ri n* (*violin*)   or
                                  バイオリン *ba i o ri n*

5 *w* sounds. These are formed in two ways:

   i ウイ (*ui*)、ウエ (*ue*)、ウオ (*uo*)
   ii ウィ (*wi*)、ウェ (*we*)、ウォ (*wo*)
                     (the second symbol is small)

Traditionally, **i** are used for loanwords and **ii** are used for foreign names and countries. However, as with **4**, in practice this is not a 'hard and fast' rule. It has become very fashionable to use the small symbols and young people in particular are tending to use them.

   i ウイスキー *u i su kī* (*whisky*)
      ウエター *u e tā* (*waiter*)
   ii ノルウェー *no ru wē* (*Norway*)
      ウォークマン *wō ku ma n* (*walkman*)

6 Combination sounds using small ア (*a*), イ (*i*), ウ (*u*), エ (*e*), オ (*o*):

In **4** and **5** these are used in forming *v* and *w* sounds. They are also used to make a number of other sounds which do not exist in Japanese but are needed for foreign words. They are easy to read if you remember that the vowel part of the first symbol is replaced with the vowel sound of the small symbol. For example:

ファ (*fa*) the *u* sound of フ (*fu*) is replaced with ア (*a*)

Now you work out these sounds:

フィ (   )   フェ (   )   フォ (   )   シェ (   )
ジェ (   )   チェ (   )   ツァ (   )   ツェ (   )
ティ (   )   ディ (   )

There are a few other sounds such as クァ (*kwa*), グァ (*gwa*) and クォ (*kwo*) but these are not used very often. Here are the sounds you should have written/worked out in the previous paragraph:

フィ (*fi*)   フェ (*fe*)   フォ (*fo*)   シェ (*she*)
ジェ (*je*)   チェ (*che*)   ツァ (*tsa*)   ツェ (*tse*)
ティ (*ti*)   ディ (*di*)*

* Sometimes this sound is represented by ジ (*ji*) ラジオ *ra ji o* (*radio*).

This activity is designed so that you can practise reading words which contain the extra sounds you have just learnt (Rules 1–6). Match the words:

a　スパゲッティ
b　チェックイン
c　ミルクシエイク
d　ミルクティー
e　ウエートレス
f　フィルム
g　イヤホーン
h　ファックス
i　フォーク
j　シルバーシート
k　スウェーデン
l　ディスコ

1　earphone(s) (　)
2　check-in (counter) (　)
3　fax (　)
4　spaghetti (　)
5　disco (　)
6　Sweden (　)
7　fork (　)
8　waitress (　)
9　milk shake (　)
10　milk tea (　)
11　(camera) film (　)
12　silver seat (seats for elderly/disabled)

Explanation: Contracted words

This is the final Explanation section – you will then be ready to put your learning into real practice! Loanwords adopted into any language often change pronunciation either to fit that language or because that is the way the word is *heard*. Take the word *Japan*, for example, which actually is sounded *Nihon* or *Nippon* in Japanese but was heard as *Japan* by early European travellers. You have already seen the ways that loanwords are adapted to fit Japanese pronunciation rules. One final way in which loanwords are adapted is by shortening or contracting them. You have already met some examples of shortened words:

ノート　(*nōto*) *notebook* (the *book* part is no longer part of the word)

Other examples of shortened words are:

テレビ　(*terebi*) *television* (*sion* is missing; *vi* is pronounced *bi*)

They can sometimes take on new or specific meanings:

サンド　(*sando*) *toasted sandwich* (from　サンドイッチ* (*sandoitchi*) meaning *sandwich*)
* サンドイッチ (small イ) is used increasingly (see p. 138)
ハムサンド　(*hamu sando*) *toasted ham sandwich*

Examples of contracted words are:

ラジカセ (*rajikase*) means *radi(o)casse(tte)* (missing parts in brackets)

マスコミ (*masukomi*) means *mass comm(unication)* or *mass media*

These types of words can cause the most confusion when you are trying to work out meanings but practice makes perfect! So try the matching activity that follows.

練習九　Activity 9

Match the カタカナ words in the left column to their *rōmaji* and English equivalents and write the appropriate letters in the brackets.

1	オートバイ ( )	a	*toire*	a	supermarket
2	トイレ　 ( )	b	*waishatsu*	b	word processor
3	ワンピース ( )	c	*wanpīsu*	c	personal computer
4	ワープロ ( )	d	*hōmu*	d	department store
5	パソコン ( )	e	*ōtobai*	e	one piece (= dress)
6	ファミコン ( )	f	*sūpā*	f	white shirt
7	ホーム　 ( )	g	*wāpuro*	g	(plat)form
8	デパート ( )	h	*famikon*	h	autobike (= motor bike)
9	スーパー ( )	i	*pasokon*	i	toilet
10	ワイシャツ ( )	j	*depāto*	j	family computer

読む練習　Reading practice

Congratulations! You have worked through the whole of カタカナ and you can now put your learning into practice. There follows a series of activites which use カタカナ words in a range of contexts which you might encounter if you visit Japan or if you watch TV programmes or videos about Japan.

練習十　Activity 10

We will begin with a coffee shop menu. These popular places sell an assortment of drinks and light Western-style meals which means the menus are written in カタカナ. Once you can read the menu, you can order your food!

```
***  ルーナ  コーヒーショップ  ***
    ホットコーヒー        500 円
    アイスコーヒー        600 円
    ミルクティー         400 円
    レモンティー         500 円
    コーカコーラ         600 円
    オレンジジュース       400 円
    ミルク            350 円
    * * * * * * * * * * * * * * * *

    サンドイッチ／サンド
      チーズ           600 円
      ハム            700 円
      ミックス          700 円

    スパゲッティ
      ナポリタン         700 円
      ミートソース        800 円

    ピザトースト         600 円
    サラダ            500 円
    パフェ            700 円
    アップルパイ         700 円
    ケーキ          500 ～ 800 円
```

1 What is the name of this coffee shop? (clue: there is a link with the moon!)
2 What two types of coffee can you buy?
3 What two types of tea can you buy?
4 How much (円 = *yen*) is Coca-Cola?
5 How much does an orange juice cost?
6 What types of sandwich filling can you order?
7 How much would you pay for a meat sauce spaghetti dish?
8 How much would a drink of milk, pizza toast and apple pie cost in total?
9 You have a maximum of 1000 yen to spend. What drink and main meal would you choose?
10 Which two desserts cost 700 yen?

練習十一　Activity 11

You learnt in the introduction to this book and to this unit that カタカナ is used a lot nowadays in advertising. This is because it has the effect of making words stand out (as we use capital letters or italics). Native Japanese words written in カタカナ require a knowledge of Japanese vocabulary to work out their meanings. In this activity you should recognize all the words because they are the names of well-known Japanese companies. Different fonts have been chosen for this activity so that you can get used to reading different styles. These styles are used frequently, for example, on neon signs. A checklist of Japanese companies written in *rōmaji* is also given – but not all appear in the activity! So now work out which companies are advertising in the signs.

1 トヨタ

2 ソニー

3 カシオ

4 ナショナル

5 サンヨー

6 ミツビシ

Checklist

Sony, Toyota, Sanyō, National, Mitsubishi, Honda, Casio, Seiko, Yamaha, Nikon, Suzuki, Kawasaki, Matsui, Subaru.

練習十二　Activity 12

Electrical stores housing the latest gadgets can be found all over Japan. Most electrical gadgets are given foreign names and so are written in カタカナ. Look at the floor plan, and answer the questions.

Floor 6	ファン、ヒーター、エアコン、トイレ
Floor 5	テレビ、ビデオ、レーザーディスク
Floor 4	ファックス、ワープロ、トイレ
Floor 3	コンピュータ、プリンター、ソフト
Floor 2	カメラ、レンズ、フィルム、トイレ
Floor 1	ＣＤプレーヤ、ステレオ、ウォークマン
Basement	ラジカセ、テープレコーダー、ラジオ

1 On which floors are the toilets?
2 Which floor do you think specializes in computer ware?
3 Besides computers, what else is sold on this floor?
4 Which floor sells air conditioners?
5 What is being sold on the fifth floor?
6 Where could you buy a camera lens?
7 Where could you buy a stereo?
8 How many floors sell audio equipment?
9 As well as word processors, what else can you buy on the fourth floor?
10 Which floor would you go to for a tape recorder?

練習十三　Activity 13

Match the currencies in the left column with the countries in the right (some may require a little guesswork!):

1	ポンド	a	フィリピン
2	ペソ	b	アメリカ
3	ユーロ	c	イギリス
4	ドル	d	スイス
5	フラン	e	インド
6	ルピー	f	イタリア

練習十四　Activity 14

There follows a list of world currency rates from a Japanese newspaper. Can you work out the countries and currencies listed? Use your answers from Activity 13 to get you started on this task. The country is given first followed immediately by the currency with no gap. You will notice that three 漢字 are included in the list, these are 米 (see Unit 6, p. 74), 英 (this is the 漢字 for *England*) and 南 (see Unit 8, p. 115). This is because many countries can be written using a 漢字 name as well as being phonetically written in katakana.

米ドル	134.65円
ユーロ	117.36
英ポンド	192.77
スイスフラン	79.65
カナダドル	84.79
メキシコペソ	15.76
オーストラリアドル	69.99
ニュージーランドドル	57.69
南アフリカランド	13.19
サウジアラビアリアル	36.49
インドルピー	2.94
タイバーツ	3.13
シンガポールドル	73.82
マレーシアリンギ	–
インドネシア100ルピア	1.43
フィリピンペソ	2.78

練習十五　Activity 15

Finally, there is a set of カタカナ signs from photographs taken in Tokyo. Can you read them and work out the English meaning? がんばって (*ganbatte*) – good luck!

1

Which famous restaurant is this?

2

カラオケ館

What activity can you do here?

3

オープニングセール

What is happening at this shop?

4

ビデオ
と
本

5

リサイクル
と環境

The two kanji mean *environment*. What are people being asked to do?

6

カレーハウス CoCo

What is CoCo?

7

バレンタインDAY

8

ビール

9

デザート

10

Eメール

11

新品台数限定品

12

トヨタ

13 シングルモルト

14 ワイン

15 クリスマスツリー

What type of tree is this?

What type of whisky is this?

16

ニコラス・ケイジ　メグ・ライアン

「ゴースト」を超える感動に全米が泣いた!

大ヒット上映中!

京都松竹座

かつて地上に存在したことのない、ピュアな恋。

シティ・オブ・エンジェル

What is the title of the film? (bottom line)
What are the actors' names? (above picture)

書く練習　Writing practice 7

This short activity is designed to help you write your name in カタカナ. A short list of popular first names follows. Try saying your name out loud and matching the appropriate カタカナ symbol to each syllable. You will need to refer back to the various rules given in this unit. For example, the name **LAURA** has the sounds *lō ra*. The nearest to these sounds are:

ローラ (*rōra*)

And CHRISTOPHER sounds out as *k ri s to phaa*. In Japanese this becomes:

クリストファー (*kurisutofā*)

If you know a Japanese person, work out your name and get them to check it. Here is a list of 20 names to help you.

ANNA	アナ	(*ana*)
CATHY	カシー	(*kashi-*)
CLARE	クレア	(*kurea*)
DIANA	ダイアナ	(*daiana*)
HILARY	ヒラリー	(*hirari-*)
JANE	ジェイン	(*jein*)
MARY	メアリー	(*meari-*)
MICHELLE	ミシェル	(*misheru*)
SARA	セーラ	(*se-ra*)
SUE	スー	(*su-*)
ANDREW	アンドリュー	(*andoryū*)
BILL	ビル	(*biru*)
BRAD	ブラッド	(*buraddo*)
GREGG	グレッグ	(*gureggu*)
JOHN	ジョン	(*jon*)
MIKE	マイク	(*maiku*)
PAUL	ポール	(*po-ru*)
ROBERT	ロバート	(*roba-to*)
STEVE	スティーブ	(*suti-bu*)
TOM	トム	(*tomu*)

終りに Conclusion

You have covered the whole of the カタカナ syllabary in this unit including the various rules and adaptations of non-Japanese words. You have had opportunities to read a wide range of words and to identify typical street signs. Hopefully you have discovered that because カタカナ is used to write non-Japanese (and often English words) it can be fun and very accessible. There is a lot to take in so treat this unit as one you can keep re-visiting and that you can enjoy! And look for opportunities to read カタカナ around you (TV programmes, newspapers, magazines, visits to Japan) so that you can impress your friends and family!

10

第十課 unit 10

In this unit you will
- **learn to read different types of text including:**
  - cooking instructions
  - cartoons
  - weather forecast
  - song lyrics
  - haiku (short poems)
- **learn the basics for reading and writing letters**

はじめに　Introduction

The aim of this unit is to pull together everything you have learnt throughout this book and apply it to reading Japanese texts. There are many types of text which use different styles of writing and have different levels of difficulty. This unit will get you started on reading and will introduce you to some techniques for accessing text which you can then build on.

Some tips on grammar functions and particles are given first and you can refer back to these as necessary. Where 漢字 appear in a text which have been introduced in earlier units, there is a short pre-activity for you to see how many you can remember. However, do not worry if you cannot remember them all, the activity is simply a device to get you thinking about what you have learnt and for making connections. Check the answers to these pre-activities in the back before proceeding and, if you want to look back to where the 漢字 was first introduced, remember that you can look up the English meaning in the index and this will refer you back to that unit.

You will be asked to mark parts of the texts as a way of identifying and separating different words and features. This is especially helpful because Japanese writing does not normally have gaps between words (as you will notice in the texts that follow). You could use different coloured highlighter pens or use different types of markings (circle, underline, overline). Or you could copy the relevant parts of the text onto paper and mark them.

Explanation: Grammar functions

Read through the information that follows but do not worry if you are not clear about all of it because the texts will have practical examples and you can then refer back to the summaries beneath the text to consolidate your learning.

Particles and sentence order

1 Every noun in a Japanese sentence is usually followed by a particle. A particle is a grammar marker which tells you the function of the noun it marks. Let us look at some examples to help you understand this. In English, the sentence order tells you the function of the main sentence parts:

I ate Japanese food
'I' is the **subject** of the sentence (who ate) and comes at the beginning of the sentence
'ate' is the **verb**
'Japanese food' is the **object** of the sentence (what I ate) and comes after the verb

This order is called SVO (subject, verb, object).

We also use particle-type words (called prepositions) such as 'with', 'by' and 'at':

*I ate Japanese food **at** home **with** chopsticks*
at marks 'home' and **with** marks 'chopsticks'. They are placed before (**pre**-position) the noun they mark.

2 This is what happens in Japanese:

私は　和食を　食べました　I Japanese cuisine ate
私 (I) is followed by the particle は. It marks the **subject** of the sentence 和食 (Japanese food) is followed by the particle を. It marks the **object** of the sentence.

The order in Japanese is SOV (subject, object, verb).

There are other particles with different functions such as で (*with*):

私は　はしで　和食を　食べました　I chopsticks with Japanese food ate

However, the order of the Japanese sentence is more flexible than the English order because the particles, not the order, tell you the functions of the different parts. So you could say:

私は　和食を　はしで　食べました　I Japanese food chopsticks with ate

But the verb **always** comes at the end of the sentence.

3 Particles are always placed **after** the noun or time expression they mark. Look at the diagram showing the key particles:

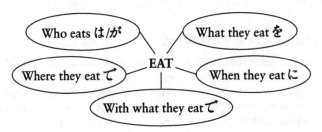

4 Particle descriptions

は (pronounced *wa* as a particle not *ha*) topic or subject marker of sentence

が (*ga*) subject marker of verb

を (*o*) object marker of sentence

で (*de*) 1 *with, by*: はしで (*with chopsticks*); 電車で (*by train*)

2 place where action happens: レストランで (*at/in the restaurant*)

に (*ni*) 1 *to* (direction): 東京に (*to Tokyo*) (also can use へ pronounced *e*)

2 *at, on* (after time): 月曜日に (*on Monday*); 一時に (*at one o'clock*)

3 *at, in, on* (place/position): 東京に住んでいます (*I live in Tokyo*)

の (*no*) 1 *of, 's*: 日本の米 (Japan's rice or *Japanese rice*)

2 links a noun with its position: 山の上 (mountain's top or *on top of the mountain*)

と (*to*) 1 *and* (between nouns): 日本と米国 (*Japan and America*)

2 *with* (accompanied by): 日本人と (*with a Japanese person*)

Quick translation tips

You will be given lots of pointers throughout this unit so this is a summary list for you to refer back to as necessary.

1 Find the topic/subject of the sentence by looking for は:

私は 本を 読みます (I book read) subject is 私 (I)

2 Then translate 'backwards' from the end of the sentence:

(私は) 本を　読みます

←————————

　book　　read

3 Describing words are generally placed in the same order as English:

私は　古い本を　読みました (I old book read)

4 In the texts that follow, both literal (*lit.*) and natural English are given to help you understand the phrases and structuring.

5 Where relevant or helpful the meaning of the 漢字 radical is given in brackets. Assume it is a left-hand radical unless stated otherwise.

練習一　Activity 1　漫画 *(Manga)*

遊More　京都精華大
大学院風刺専攻　小川　信子

「たしかに『もっと本を読みなさい』
とは言ったけど…

漫画 *(manga* – 'cartoon') and アニメ *(anime)* or animation are very popular in Japan and are known around the world. Cartoon books fill bookshops and kiosk shelves and Japanese people of all ages can be seen reading them on trains, in bookshops and at home. The one-frame cartoon here is taken from the *Kyoto News*, a Japanese newspaper. It is from the education section and is a joke about 教育ママ *(kyōiku mama)* or 'education mothers' who go to great lengths to ensure their children study hard and get into the best schools. Now work through the series of activities starting with a review.

1　漢字復習　Kanji review

There are three 漢字 in the cartoon and you have learnt them all! Do you remember them? They are:

a 本　**b** 読　**c** 言

2　Find and mark these ひらがな words:

a たしかに *(tashika ni)* certainly, indeed
b もっと *(motto)* more
c けど *(kedo)* but

3 Mark these particles and grammar functions:

a を (*o*) object marker

b ...なさい (*nasai*) verb ending indicating a command, in this case 'read!'

c ...とは (*to wa*) used in reported speech (I said that...). は adds emphasis (I **did** say...)

d 「 indicates open quote mark (close quote mark is 」). 『』 means quote within a quote.

4 **翻訳** *Honyaku*   **Translation**

「たしかに...とは言った   '*Indeed I did say...*
『もっと本を読みなさい』   "*Read more books!*"
けど...   *but...*'

The 'but' trails off, the reader fills in the rest from the picture ('but this is ridiculous!').

Notice the technique of translating the information outside the double quotes first then adding the part in double quotes. This would be the order in which we would say it in English whereas in Japanese the 'I said' part comes at the end. Emphasis on たしかに (*indeed*) is achieved by placing it at the beginning.

練習二　Activity 2　Cookery instructions

イラスト　まつもと　きなこ

The sequence is from the children's educational section of a newspaper. There are two sets of simple cooking instructions.

1 漢字復習 Kanji review

Write down the English meanings of these 漢字 and カタカナ words:

a 水 (*mizu*)   b 玉 (*tama*)   c 火 (*hi*)   d 指 (*yubi*)
e テスト   f ティシュ   g フライパン

Now mark them in the text. Remember to check your answers in the back before proceeding.

2 Title: 卵をわる (top three pictures)

a Find and mark these 漢字:

卵 (*tamago*) egg   角 (*kado*) corner, edge   当て (*ate*) hit
親指 (*oya yubi*) thumb (*lit.: parent finger*)

b Find and mark these ひらがな words:

わる (*waru*) break   かたい (*katai*) hard
われめ (*wareme*) a crack   あてて (*atete*) put
まえ (= 前 *mae*) front   うしろ (= 後ろ *ushiro*) back
ねじる (*nejiru*) twist

c Find and mark these カタカナ words:

コンコン (*konkon*) tap tap (sound)
ポトン (*poton*) with a plop (sound)

d Mark these particles. Remember that particles are positioned after the word they mark:

を   (*o*) positioned after the object of the sentence – the object marker (appears two times)
に   (*ni*) to, in, on (appears three times)
と   (*to*) with (placed after the word); and (placed between two nouns)

e 翻訳 *Honyaku*   Translation

Title 卵をわる	Breaking an egg
かたい角に	on a hard edge
コンコンと当て	hit with a tap tap
われめに	in the crack
親指をあてて	put (your) thumb
まえとうしろにねじる	twist to the front and back (forwards and backwards)

3 Title: 水玉テスト (lower three pictures – excluding thought bubble)

a Find and mark these 漢字:

油 (*abura*) oil
水玉 (*mizutama*) water ball/drop
指先 (*yubisaki*) fingertip
置き (*oki*) place
落とす (*otosu*) drop
十分 (*jūbun*) enough

b Find and mark these ひらがな and カタカナ words:

たたんだもの (*tatanda mono*) folded (thing)
のばす (*nobasu*) spread
つけて (*tsukete*) switch on, apply (appears twice)
あたためる (温める = *atatameru*) warm up (also appears
as あたたまている)
ころがったら (*korogattara*) if (it) rolls
しるし (*shirushi*) sign
じゅつ (*ju*) ping
コンロ (*konro*) hob

c Mark these particles and grammar functions:

を (*o*) object marker (appears five times)
で (*de*) with, by means of
に (*ni*) on, into (three times)
て (*te*) verb ending meaning *and*
が (*ga*) subject marker
たら (*tara*) verb ending meaning *if, when*

d 翻訳 *Honyaku* — Translation

Title 水玉テスト	Water drop test
ティシュをたたんだもので	with a folded tissue
油をのばす	spread the oil
フライパンをコンロに置き	place the frying pan on the hob
火をつけてあたためる	switch on the heat (fire) and warm up
指先に水をつけて	apply water to the fingertip and
フライパンに落とす	drop into the frying pan
水玉がころがったら	if (when) the water drop rolls
十分あたたまってい るしるし	(it's) a sign that it is warmed up enough.

練習三 Activity 3 How to make green tea

The sequence of four instructions on the tea packet (p. 158) show you how to make perfect Japanese green tea. Once you can read them, you can try making green tea for yourself!

1 漢字復習 Kanji review

Write down the English meanings of these 漢字 words. Then mark them in the text and write down how many times each appears.

a 飲 b 人 c 目 d 入 e お茶
f 便 g 大 h 出 i 時

2 General points

Here are some general words used throughout the text which are useful to look at first. They will be referred to again in the translations so use this list as a reference list.

〜分 (- *bun*) means *share, part, per*. 3人分 means *three people's worth* or *three helpings* (food)

〜目 (- *me*) means *-th, -rd, -nd* as in 4つ目 (*fourth*). 1煎目 means *first infusion*

* 分 (*fun*) also means *minute*. 2分 means *two minutes*.

The vocabulary and translation is now introduced section by section. Once introduced, vocabulary is not repeated in later sections so you will need to refer back as necessary.

Picture 1

3a Find and mark these 漢字:

飲み方 (*nomikata*) how to drink
人数 (*ninzū*) number of people
分 (*bun*) part, per   湯 (*yu*) hot water
湯呑み (alternative: 湯飲み = *yu nomi*) teacup
〜分目 (*bunme*) parts   温度 (*ondo*) temperature
約 (*yaku*) approximately
湯ざまし (*yuzamashi*) hot water cooler
代りに (*kawari*) in place of, instead of
使用する (*shiyō suru*) use
便利 (*benri*) convenient, handy

b Find and mark these ひらがな words:

おいしい (*oishii*) delicious   ほど (*hodo*) about
入れてさきます (*irete samashimasu*) put in and cool

おいしい飲み方

人数分の湯呑みにお湯を
8分目ほど入れてさまします。
お湯の温度約80℃

　湯呑みを湯ざましの代りに
使用すると便利です。

お茶の葉を急須に入れます。
3人分で6〜8g
（大さじ約1.5杯分）

湯呑みのお湯を急須にあけて、茶葉に
お湯が浸透するのを待ちます。
浸出時間約1分
（濃いお茶が好きな人は
長めに）

※2煎目の浸出時間は約10秒
　（1煎目より熱いお湯を使用）

お茶を注ぐ分量は均等に、
お茶は最後の
一滴まで絞りきりましょう。

c Mark these particles and grammar functions:

の (*no*) between two nouns indicates that the second noun
  belongs to the first (× 3)
に (*ni*) into, in (× 2)
お (*o*) before a noun makes the word sound more honorific.
  お湯 (× 2)
を (*o*) object marker (× 2)
と (*to*) if (× 1)

d 翻約 *Honyaku* Translation

Match the Japanese on the left with the translation on the
right. The first is done for you:

1 おいしい飲み方 (title)	i If you use teacups . . . ( )
2 人数分の湯呑みに	ii it is handy ( )
3 お湯を8分目ほど入	iii instead of a water cooler ( )
れてきましす。	iv the temperature of the hot
4 お湯の温度約80°C	water is about 80°C ( )
5 湯呑みを . . . . 使用	v a delicious drinking method
すると	(1)
6 湯ざましの代りに	vi put in about eight parts hot
7 便利です	water and cool ( )
	vii into drinking cups per
	number of people ( )

Picture 2

4a Find and mark these 漢字:

葉 (*ha*) leaves   急須 (*kyūsu*) teapot
3人分 (*sanninbun*) 3 helpings
大さじ (*ōsaji*) tablespoon   約 (see a))
杯分 (*haibun*) cupful/spoonful

b Circle the particle で (*de*) meaning 'for'; の × 1; を × 1; に × 1

c 翻訳 *Honyaku*   Translation

お茶の葉を急須に入れます。	Put the tea leaves in the teapot
3人分で 6-8g	for three helpings (people) (it is) 6–8 grams
(大さじ約1・5杯分)	(in tablespoons (it's) approximately 1.5 spoonfuls)

Picture 3

5a Find and mark these 漢字:

浸透する (*shintō suru*) brew, permeate
待ちます (*machimasu*) wait
侵出 (*shinshutsu*) brewing
時間 (*jikan*) time   **1分** (*ippun*) 1 minute
濃い (*koi*) strong, dark
好きな人 (*sukina hito*) people who like
長めに (*nagame ni*) lengthen
 1煎目 (*ichimaeme*) the first infusion
10秒 (*jūbyō*) 10 seconds   熱い (*atsui*) hot

b Mark these particles and grammar functions:

お (honorific) × 4; の × 3; に × 3; を × 3; が × 2; は × 2
より (*yori*) *than* (placed after)

c 翻訳 *Honyaku* Translation

Match the Japanese on the left with the correct translation
on the right:

1	湯呑みのお湯を	i the hot water on the tea leaves ( )
2	急須にあけて	ii lengthen (the time) ( )
3	茶葉にお湯が	iii put in the teapot ( )
4	浸透するのを 待ちます	iv wait for it (the hot water . . .) to brew ( )
5	浸出時間約1分	v people who like strong tea ( )
6	濃いお茶が好き な人は	vi the hot water in the teacups ( )
7	長めに	vii brewing time (is) about 1 minute ( )

Asterisked part: *the brewing time for the second infusion (refill) is about 10 seconds*

2nd Bracketed part: *use hot water that is hotter than for the first infusion*

Picture 4

6a Find and mark these 漢字:

注ぐ (*sosogu*) pour into   分量 (*bunryō*) quantity
均等に (*kintō ni*) uniformly   最後 (*saigo*) final
一滴 (*itteki*) one drop   絞り (*shibori*) squeeze, extract

b Grammar points:

まで (*made*) up to
～きりましょう (*kirimashō*) let's finish . . .

c 翻訳 *Honyaku*   Translation

| お茶を注ぐ分量は均等に | pour the quantity of tea uniformly |
| お茶は . . . 絞りきりましょう 最後の一滴まで | (let's) squeeze out the tea to the final drop |

練習四 Activity 4

天気予報 *(Tenki yohō)* The weather forecast

The weather forecast shown on p. 162 is taken from the Kyoto newspaper. Its title (top left-hand corner) is:

きょうの天気 *(kyō no tenki)* Today's weather

1 漢字復習 Kanji review

Decode the place names that follow (refer to map of Japan in Unit 8, p. 116):

a 大阪   **b** 東京   **c** 札幌   **d** 京都

Now find them on the weather report (look at the left side of the text) and mark them (京都 appears four times).

2 Key

Below the written text (beginning **29** 日 . . .) there is a key consisting of two boxes. Can you see them?

The box with the straight line in the middle indicates のち *(nochi)* which means *later*. For example: ✳️◼️ means 'sunny later cloudy'.

The box with the slanting line indicates 時々／一時 *(tokodoki ichiji)* meaning *sometimes / for a time*. For example: ✳️◼️ 'sometimes sunny, for a time cloudy'.

3 Look at the left-hand column (きょうの天気)

a Find these place names:

福井 Fukui   福岡 Fukuoka   神戸 Kobe   奈良 Nara 名古屋 Nagoya   鹿児島 Kagoshima

Now answer these questions from the information given in the left-hand column.

b What is the weather going to be like in:

   i Tokyo   **ii** Osaka   **iii** Fukui   **iv** Kagoshima?

c Name two other cities where it will be:

   i cloudy then sunny   **ii** sunny then cloudy

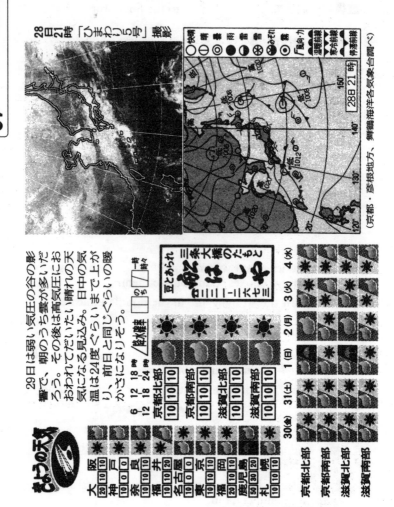

4 **Middle and lower picture-symbol columns**

a 漢字復習 (Kanji review). Write down the meanings of these 漢字:

i 北　　ii 南　　iii 金　　iv 土
v 月　　vi 火　　vii 水

iii–vii also represent the days of the week. Which days do they represent? (see Unit 1, p. 5). Check your answers in the back then find them in the text.

b You should have identified 京都 (Kyoto) four times in these columns. The other place name (also mentioned four times) is 滋賀 (Shiga). After both these place names are these 漢字: 北部 (*hokubu*) and 南部 (*nanbu*). 部 means *part*, therefore 'north part' and 'south part' (of the Kyoto and Shiga areas). The middle column is today's weather, the lower column is the forecast for the 30th–4th. Now answer these questions.

c What is today's weather like in:

i the north part of Kyoto (area)
ii the south part of Shiga (area)
iii the south part of Kyoto (area)?

d What is the weather forecast for:

i south Kyoto on Friday
ii south Kyoto on Tuesday
iii north Kyoto on Sunday
iv north Shiga on Saturday
v south Shiga on Wednesday
vi north Kyoto on Monday?

e On which day and where might you need an umbrella? (Two answers)

5 **Right-side pictures** (top and bottom)

a 日 preceded by a number indicates a date.
3 日 means *3rd* (day).
時 preceded by a number indicates 'o'clock'.
3 時 means *3 o'clock*.

Look at the top satellite picture. When was it taken? (time and date)

b The lower picture has a number of circular symbols to the right followed by 漢字. You learnt most of these in

Units 6 and 7. Can you identify them now? They are quite small, the size of a real newspaper:

  i 晴   ii 雲 (also look up 雲)
iii 雨   iv 雷   v 雪

Look back to the previous units if you need to, then check your answers in the back and mark the terms in the text (some are quite small).

c There are four other circular symbols with weather terms. Find and mark them:

快晴 *good weather*   霧 *mist, fog*
風向.力 *wind direction/strength*   みぞれ *sleet*

6 The text

A short text is located above the picture–symbol columns. Go through steps 1–4 that follow then try your own translation before looking at step 5 (the translation).

  i Find and highlight the following 漢字 words and phrases. What do they mean?

    a 29日   **b** 雲   **c** 高
    d 晴れ   **e** 天気   **f** 上

  ii Find and highlight the following 漢字 words and phrases:

    a 弱い (*yowai*) weak
    b 気圧 (*kiatsu*) atmospheric pressure
    c 谷 (*tani*) valley (trough)
    d 影響 (*eikyō*) influence, effect
    e 朝 (*asa*) morning
    f 多い (*ooi*) many
    g その後 (*sono go*) after that
    h 高気圧 (*kōkiatsu*) high pressure
    i 見込み (*mikomi*) expectation
    j 日中 (*nitchū*) all day
    k 気温 (*kion*) temperature
    l 度 (*do*) degrees
    m 上がり (*agari*) to rise
    n 前日 (*zenjitsu*) previous day
    o 同じ (*onaji*) same
    p 暖かさ (*atatakasa*) warmth

  iii Find and mark these ひらがな words:

    a うち (*uchi*) during
    b だろう (*darō*) will probably

c ... におおわれて (*ni oowarete*) be covered by (literal translation)
d だいたい (*daitai*) generally
e ... になる (*ni naru*) become ...
f ぐらい (*gurai*) about (× 2)
g まで (*made*) up to
h ... になりそう (*ni narisō*) it looks like it will be (come) ... (そう = seem, look like)

iv Find and mark these particles and grammar functions:

は (*wa*) topic marker (× 3)   の (*no*) of, 's (× 7)
で (*de*) through, by means of (× 1)
が (*ga*) subject marker (× 1)   と (*to*) as (× 1)

ヒント *Hint*: Try to translate the text yourself before working through step 5. Remember: find the topic or subject then work through the sentence/phrase from the end.

v 翻訳 *Honyaku*   Translation

29日は	The 29th
弱い気圧の谷の影響で	(start from the end of this sentence and work backwards): through the influence (because of the effect) of a trough of low (weak) pressure
朝のうち	during the morning
雲が多いだろう	the clouds will probably be many (there will be a lot of cloud)
その後は ... 見込み	after that ... it is expected (that)
高気圧におおわれて	high pressure will spread and
だいたい晴れの天気になる	generally it will be (come) fine weather
日中の気温は 24度ぐらいまで上がり	the daytime temperature will rise up to about 24 degrees
... になりそう	it looks like it will be
前日と同じぐらいの暖かさ	about the same warmth as the previous day (yesterday)

練習五 **Activity 5**

手紙 *(Tegami)* **Letters**

This section will get you first to read a letter which is handwritten, and then will give you some tips for writing a letter yourself!

This letter is written downwards and you start reading at the top right, down the column. This is the traditional way of writing letters but many Japanese people nowadays write in Western style, horizontally from left to right. Writing downwards can give a letter a more formal or traditional tone. This is a New Year's greetings card and as this is a traditional custom, such cards are often (but not always) written in the traditional downwards style.

New Year cards, like Christmas cards in the West, are sent by all Japanese people to a wide range of friends, acquaintances, colleagues and clients. They normally have a short greeting but this card has been sent by a Japanese friend to a friend in England and is a combined New Year's greeting card and letter.

1 Start by identifying and marking 漢字 you have already been introduced to. As before, see how many you can remember then check the answers in the back before proceeding further.

a 新年	b 明	c 手	d 読	e 昨	f 日本
g 目	h 時	i 行	j 思	k 会	l 楽
m 気	n 年	o 旦	p 山本	q 子	

2 Find and mark these set phrases and read the explanations:

   a お目にかかれて *(o-me ni kakarete)* lit. 'I was able to set eyes on you'. This is a respectful way of saying 'I was able to see/meet you'.

   b ...楽しみに *(tanoshimi ni)* I am looking forward to ... This phrase ends with に. The full sentence would end with しています *(shiteimasu)* but this is often omitted.

   c お元気で *(o-genki de)* Take care!

3 Now mark these 漢字 words and phrases.

   a 明けまして *(akemashite)* to dawn (from 明ける *(akeru)*)
   b お手紙 *(o-tegami)* letter
   c 夫 *(otto)* husband
   d 昨年 *(sakunen)* last year
   e 写真 *(shashin)* photograph
   f 送ります *(okurimasu)* send

新年

明けまして おめでとう ございます

お手紙 ありがとう ございました。 昨年は 日本で
読ませて いただきました。 ヘレンに お目にかかれて うれしかった です。
その時の写真を <u>送</u>ります。 来年の夏は
イギリスに 行きたいと 思っています。
又、お会いできることを 楽しみに。
それでは お元気で。

一九九九年 元旦

山本 花子

g 来年 (*rainen*) next year
h 夏 (*natsu*) summer
i 又 (*mata*) again
j 元旦 (*gantan*) New Year's Day
k 花子 Hanako (girl's name. 花 means 'flower')

4 Next mark these ひらがな words and phrases:

a おめでとうございます
(*omedetō gozaimasu*) congratulations
b ありがとうございました (*arigatō gozaimashita*) thank you (for what you have done)
c うれしく (*ureshiku*) happily うれしかった (*ureshikatta*) was/were happy
d いただきました (*itadakimashita*) received (see 6c this section)
e できる (*dekiru*) be able to
f それでは (*sore dewa*) and so, well, finally (used at end of letter)

5 Mark these two カタカナ words:

a ヘレン (*heren*) Helen   b イギリス (*Igirisu*) England

6 Find and mark these particles and grammar functions:

a お (*o*) adds tone of respect to nouns (put before the word) (× 2; also see 2a and c above).
b と (*to*) and, with (see also k below).
c 読ませて (*yomasete*) (you) let me read + いただきました (I received), *lit.* 'I received you letting me read'. It is a polite way of acknowledging something which someone has done for you. Another example is: 休ませていただきました (*yasumasete itadakimashita*) '(You) let me take a break'.
d は (*wa*) topic marker (× 2).
e で (*de*) in, at (particle used to mark the place (where something happens).
f に (*ni*) with, to (× 2; also see 2a this section).
g その (*sono*) that.
h の (*no*) see notes at beginning of unit (× 2).
i を (*o*) object marker (× 2).
j 行きたい (*ikitai*) I want to go (たい = want to).
k と思っています (. . . *to omotteimasu*) I think that . . . (と here means 'that').
l こと (*koto*) placed after a verb this can be translated as ' . . . ing'. Therefore: できること (*dekiru koto*) being able to.

This time you are going to do some of the work! The translation follows, phrase by phrase. It is not in order, however, and your task is to work out the correct order. Some of it may be obvious from the English (!) but keep referring back to the text and points (1–6) of this section so that you get a good understanding of how the letter is structured.

a *lit.* 'Next year's summer I think that I want to go to England' = Next summer I hope to . . . / would like to . . .

b With my husband (my husband and I) read your letter happily (with pleasure).

c I look forward to being able to meet again.

d Thank you for your letter.

e I am sending (you) the photographs of (/from) that time.

f Well, take care.

g *lit.* 'the new year has dawned, congratulations' = Happy New Year!

h New Year's Day, 1999. (From) Hanako Yamamoto (*in Japanese, surname precedes first name*).

i I was happy that last year I was able to meet with Helen in Japan. (The Japanese often use your name instead of saying 'you'.)

書く練習 Writing letters

1 Let's start by looking at some of the features of the letter you have just read.

a Did you notice that the date is written at the end of the letter, and is followed by the name of the writer? This is standard practice.

b Hanako (the writer) begins with a greeting, in this case 'Happy New Year'. You will learn some more seasonal greetings in the next section.

c Hanako then says thank you for the letter she received. You can use this structure to thank someone for something they have sent you such as:

プレゼント *present*; はがき *postcard*; カード *card*

Just add ありがとうございました (*thank you*) after the item.

d Hanako brings the letter to a close with それでは、お元気で (*Well, take care*).

2 Now let us look at useful phrases and techniques you can use to write a letter to a Japanese friend.

a Begin with their name followed by さん (*san*) if you know the person well or さま (*sama*) for a very formal letter. In this case you might use the surname. For example:

花子さん (*Hanako san*)
山本さま (*Yamamoto-sama*) (or 花子さま *Hanako-sama*)

b Rather than beginning with an enquiry about a person's health ('How are you?') the Japanese tend to comment on the weather first and then maybe a comment about the person's health. Here are some useful phrases for different times of the year:

良いお年を (*yoi o-toshi o*) Have a good year (normally used before New Year's day).

明けましておめでとう Happy New Year (used during New Year).

メリークリスマス (*merī kurisumasu*) Merry Christmas.

まだまだ寒さが続いています (*mada mada samusa ga tsuzuiteimasu*) The cold weather continues.

ようやく春がきました (*yōyaku haru ga kimashita*) At last spring has come.

きびしい暑さが続いています (*kibishii atsusa ga tsuzuiteimasu*) The unrelenting heat continues.

静かに秋がやってきています (*shizuka ni aki ga yatte kiteimasu*) Autumn has crept up on us quietly.

c Enquiries about health: お元気ですか (*o-genki desu ka*) How are you? (informal) お元気でお過しでしょうか (*o-genki de o-sugoshi deshō ka*) How are you? (formal)

d Closing phrases:

Either: それでは、お元気で (see 1d this section) Well, take care.

Or: では、お体に気をつけて (*dewa, o-karada ni ki o tsukete*) Well, take care of yourself.
お返事お待ちしています (*o-henji o-machi shiteimasu*) I wait for your reply
きょうなら (*sayōnara*) Goodbye.
かしこ (*kashiko*) sincerely (used by women; formal).

e You don't need to use an equivalent of 'Dear' or 'from' when writing a letter. The person's name plus さん/さま (see 2a this section) and you own name at the end (after the date) is enough.

If you are writing a brief note or postcard, you can miss out the seasonal greetings and closing phrases and use this pair of phrases instead: 前略 (*zenryaku*) Greetings! (used at the beginning); 早々 (*sō sō*) Excuse the rush (used at the end).

練習六 Activity 6

さくら (*Sakura*) The cherry blossom song

This is perhaps the most well-known Japanese song. The music is reproduced as well (p. 172), so that you can try singing it once you have studied its meaning! Notice that the lyrics are written in ひらがな so that it is clear which sound fits which note.

Here are the words of the song, this time with 漢字 as well. The *rōmaji* is written to the side. You could write the *rōmaji* below the ひらがな on the music but try instead to read the ひらがな because this will be very good reading practice! Here is the text:

桜、桜	*Sakura, Sakura*
野山も郷も	*noyama mo sato mo*
見渡す限り	*miwatasu kagiri*
霞か雲か	*kasumi ka kumo ka*
朝日に匂う	*asahi ni niou*
桜、桜	*Sakura, Sakura*
花盛り	*hanazakari*

1 What are the meanings of the following 漢字:

    a 山   **b** 見
    c 雲   **d** 朝 (Unit 10, p. 164, iie)
    e 日   **f** 花 (Unit 10, p. 168)

2 Find and mark these 漢字 words:

    a 桜 (*sakura*) cherry blossom (× 4)
    b 野山 (*noyama*) fields and hills
    c 郷 (*sato*) home town
    d 見渡す (*miwatasu*) survey the scene, look out over
    e 限り (*kagiri*) endless, everywhere; as far as
    f 霞 (*kasumi*) mist (notice the rain radical)
    g 朝日 (*asahi*) morning sun
    h 匂う (*niou*) be fragrant
    i 花盛り (*hanazakari*) (flowers) in full bloom

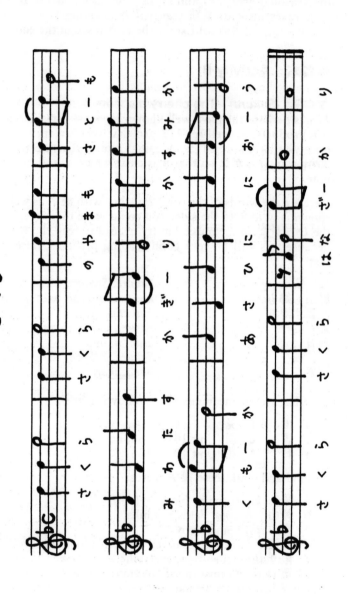

ラップ

3 Find and mark these particles and grammar functions:

a も ... も (*mo* ... *mo*) both ... and
b か ... か (*ka* ... *ka*) either ... or
c に (*ni*) in

This time you are going to try the translation completely by yourself! Song lyrics and poems often use very minimal language, and use words to evoke a sense of what is being described rather than spelling it all out. When translating into English, there are a number of stages to follow:

i Translate individual words and phrases (here done for you).
ii Put together in 'literal' English.
iii Consider what meanings are being conveyed and change into a more natural English structure.
iv At this stage, translators need to decide whether it is more important to keep closely to the original Japanese or to 'interpret' the text and put their own individual mark on it. This may depend on the text or on the purpose of the translation. Certainly with poems and songs it may be necessary to change words in order to make the song fit the tune or for the poem to retain its structure, rhythm or rhyme.

In the case of this song, however, you will be singing it in Japanese so focus on conveying the sense of the Japanese words in more natural English (but why not have a go at getting the English to fit the tune too!). There is a sample translation at the back so that you can check for meaning but as long as the meaning is correct, other versions are equally acceptable.

練習七 Activity 7 俳句 Haiku

Haiku were developed in Japan but nowadays are known and written all over the world. They are a style of poetic writing using a small number of words to convey a much deeper feeling or emotion. Traditionally the poems were observations of nature which would evoke a strong sense of the scene described or of the emotions underlying it. Modern haiku explore many themes and continue to be popular both in Japan and internationally.

A haiku traditionally is a 17-syllable poem of three lines: 5–7–5 (5 syllables, 7 syllables, 5 syllables). The four great masters of Japanese haiku were Bashō (1644–94), Buson (1716–84), Issa (1762–1826) and Shiki (1867–1902). A few haiku by these great masters follow – you are going to have a go at translating

173

unit 10 第十課

10

them! A choice of English translations of a word will often be given so that you can 'experiment' with your translation. There are sample translations at the back so that you can check on meanings. Most translators try to capture the sense of the poem in English without retaining the 5–7–5 form but once you have the meaning you could try to reduce it to 17 syllables!

I

涼しさや	*suzushisa ya*	子規	Shiki
青田の中に	*aota no naka ni*		
一つ松	*hitotsu matsu*		

1 You have met these 漢字 in this book. What do they mean?

    a 青   **b** 田   **c** 中   **d** 一

2 The new 漢字 words are:

    a 涼しき (*suzushisa*) coolness (water radical)
    b 松 (*matsu*) pine tree (tree radical)

3 Particles and grammar functions

    a や (*ya*) A poetic convention, for emphasis translated as 'the' or 'a' (like は *wa*) Some translators use . . . after the word to set the scene. For example: 涼しさや The coolness . . .
    b の (*no*) of   **c** に (*ni*) in
    d 一つ (*hitotsu*) one (item); a single (thing)

II

古池や	*furuike ya*	芭蕉	Bashō
蛙飛び込む	*kawazu tobikomu*		
水の音	*mizu no oto*		

1 You have met these 漢字 in this book. What do they mean?

    a 古   **b** 水   **c** 音

2 The new 漢字 words are:

    a 池 (*ike*) pond (*water* radical)
    b 蛙 (*kawazu*) frog (*insect* radical)
    c 飛び込む (*tobikomu*) leap / plunge / dive / jump into

3 Particles and grammar functions:

    a や (*ya*) see 3a above   **b** の (*no*) of

III

夕風や	*yūkaze ya*	蕪村	Buson
水青鷺の	*mizu aosagi no*		
脛を打つ	*hagi o utsu*		

1 You have met these 漢字 in this book. What do they mean?

   a 風 (p. 164, 5c)   **b** 水   **c** 青

2 The new 漢字 words are:

   a 夕 (*yū*) evening
   b 鷺 (*sagi*) heron (*bird* radical, below)
   c 脛 (*hagi*) leg, shin (*flesh* radical)
   d 打つ (*utsu*) hit, knock/lap against (*hand* radical)

3 The particles and grammar functions are:

   a や (*ya*) see 3a   **b** の (*no*) of
   c を (*o*) object marker

IV

秋の夜や	*aki no yo ya*	一茶　Issa
旅の男の	*tabi no otoko no*	
針仕事	*hari shigoto*	

1 You have met these 漢字 in this book. What do they mean?

   a 旅   **b** 男   **c** 針

2 The new 漢字 words are:

   a 秋 (*aki*) autumn   **b** 夜 (*yo*) night
   c 仕事 (*shigoto*) work

3 The particles and grammar functions are:

   a や (*ya*) see I, 3a   **b** の (*no*) of, connects linked words

終りに　Conclusion

おめでとうございます (*omedetō gozaimasu*) *Congratulations*! You have completed *Teach Yourself Beginner's Japanese Script*. I hope that you now feel you have a good grounding in Japanese reading and writing and are ready to take your study further and tackle new challenges! Look for every opportunity to use your learning so that you can consolidate it, and re-visit the units in this book to refresh your learning. If you have not yet tackled the spoken language or only have the basics, then how about trying *Teach Yourself Beginner's Japanese* next? And please write to me (c/o Hodder and Stoughton) to let me know how you got on with this book.

それでは、さようなら!

key to the activities

Unit 1

Work it out!

1 c, 2 g, 3 h, 4 i, 5 a, 6 1, 7 f, 8 j, 9 e, 10 k, 11 b, 12 d.

Activity 1

a 6, b 14, c 10, d 9, e 11, f 12, g 3, h 2, i 13, j 1, k 7, l 14, m 8, n 5.

Activity 2

a 5, b 1, c 4, d 7, e 6, f 3, g 2.

Activity 3

1 Wed　2 Tues　3 Sun　4 Fri　5 Sat　6 2　7 1　8 2　9 Mon.

Unit 2

Work it out!

1 l, 2 k, 3 g, 4 e, 5 d, 6 a, 7 c, 8 b, 9 h, 10 i, 11 j, 12 f.

Activity 1

a 6, b 2, c 3, d 4, e 8, f 9, g 10, h 1, i 7, j 5.

Activity 2

1　a Sun　b Wed　c Mon　d Sat.
2　4 (4th, 11th, 18th, 25th).
3　Sun.

Activity 3

1 April, March.
2 **a** April, July **b** June, Feb, March **c** Sept, Dec.
3 **a** Sun **b** Sat **c** Tues **d** Wed **e** Wed.
4 **a** Mon **b** Wed **c** Sun **d** Mon–Sun **e** Mon.

Activity 4

a Sat 14th Feb   **b** Thurs 20th Nov
c Mon 5th May   **d** Sun 10th Sept
e Wed 25th Dec   **f** Fri 1st April.

Activity 6

  i 1 b, 2 c, 3 b, 4 a, 5 c
 ii 1 a, 2 c, 3 b, 4 a, 5 c;
iii 1 c,ii 2 a,iii 3 c,i 4 b,ii 5 b,i 6 a,iii
        7 b,i 8 c,i 9 a,iii 10 a,ii.

Activity 7

a Hayashi   **b** Morita   **c** Moriyama   **d** Yamakawa
e Takeyama   **f** Mori   **g** Kita   **h** Ishikawa
i Kaneda   **j** Takeda   **k** Ishida   **l** Yamada
m Kawada.

Test

1 **a** man **b** wood **c** power **d** gold.
2 **a** population **b** Japan **c** girl **d** gateway
   e volcano **f** men and women.
3 **a** ii **b** vi **c** vii **d** v **e** i **f** iii **g** iv.
4 **a** Yamada **b** Takeyama **c** Morita **d** Mori **e** Ishida.
5 check writing sections/charts.

Unit 3

Introduction

a iii **b** iv **c** ii.

Activity 1

1 **a** iv **b** vi **c** v **d** i **e** ii **f** iii. 3 **a** 6, **b** 4, **c** 5, **d** 8.

Activity 2

3 h, g, b, e, i, c, d, f, a, j.
4 **a** 9 **b** 6 **c** 7 **d** 19 **e** 17 **f** 13 **g** 20 **h** 50 **i** 70
   j 21 **k** 32 **l** 43 **m** 54 **n** 65 **o** 76 **p** 87 **q** 88 **r** 99.

Activity 3

1 e, f, b, d, c, h, g, a; 600.
2 **a** 8000 **b** 5000 **c** 7000 **d** 6000 **e** 2000 **f** 1000.
3 **a** iii **b** i **c** iv **d** ii **e** v.
4 a, e, b, g, d, c, f. 200; 2000; 2200; 20,000; 200,000;
   2,000,000; 20,000,000.
5 **a** ii **b** v **c** vii **d** vi **e** iv **f** i **g** iii.

Activity 4

1 1 b, 2 e, 3 a, 4 d, 5 c.
2 1 d, 2 c, 3 f, 4 e, 5 b, 6 a.
3 **1** 11th Nov **2** 18th June **3** 2nd Oct **4** 21st Aug
   5 31st Mar **6** 24th June.

Activity 5

1 **a** iv **b** v **c** vi **d** i **e** iii **f** ii.
2 **a** iii **b** v **c** iv **d** i **e** vi **f** ii.

Activity 6

1 **a** (03) 358–1377   **b** (097) 592–4211
   c (0720) 21–3866   **d** (03) 3593–2704
   e (0279) 221–3154.
2 **a** Sat 5th Dec 1998   **b** Sun 6th Dec 1998
   c Sat 12th Dec 1998.
3 Sat 21st Oct 1995.

Unit 4

Introduction

1 **a** mouth **b** ear **c** person **d** eye **e** mountain
   f gate **g** tree **h** sun(day) **i** child.
2 **a** gate and ear **b** eye **c** sun **d** mouth **e** child **f** eye
   g tree **h** mountain.

Activity 1

a 4, b 2, c 7, d 6, e 5, f 1, g 3.

Activity 2

1 f, 2 g, 3 e, 4 a, 5 d, 6 b, 7 c.

Activity 4

1 b, 2 e, 3 f, 4 g, 5 a, 6 d, 7 c.

Activity 5

1 e, 2 b, 3 g, 4 f, 5 d, 6 a, 7 c.

Activity 6

1 f, 2 b, 3 c, 4 d, 5 a, 6 e.

Activity 7

1 f, 2 e, 3 b, 4 g, 5 c, 6 a, 7 d.

Activity 8

1 dealer   2 entrance   3 exit   4 drinking water
5 academic ability   6 buyer   7 holiday   8 Japanese person.

Activity 9

1   1 d, 2 e, 3 f, 4 h, 5 k, 6 i, 7 m, 8 b, 9 c, 10 d, 11 j, 12 g,
    13 l, 14 a.
2   a baibai   b dokusho   c nyūgaku   d shutsunyū   e inshoku
    f kengaku   g kyūgaku   h kenbun.

Test

1   a horse   b person   c woman   d man   e child   f girl
    g boy   h Japanese person.
2   a mountain   b volcano   c river   d water   e fire   f tree
    g wood   h forest   i rice field.
3   a 1   b 5   c 60 yen   d 100   e 4000 yen   f 20,000
    g gold, money   h 3700.
4   a Sat 11th Sept   b 20th August   c 1991 (year)
    d *Heisei* 12th year = Year 2000.
5   a listen   b eat   c drink   d say   e talk   f read   g sell
    h look   i buy   j rest.
6   a ear   b mouth   c foot   d eye   e hand.

Unit 5

Introduction

1   to write grammar and non-漢字 Japanese words.
2   ひらがな.
3   simplified 漢字 with the same pronunciation.
4   46.

Work it out!

(Reading down): d, f, a, c, b, e.

Activity 1

a sushi **b** aki **c** koe **d** tsukue **e** satou/satō **f** seito.

Activity 2

7 a 1 **b** 2 **c** 2. **8** け. **9** す. **15 a** 2 **b** 2. **16** 10. **17** ほ.

Activity 3

Set 1 **a** asa **b** te **c** natsu **d** tokei **e** shio **f** nani **g** nuno.
Set 2 **a** yoru **b** mimi **c** haru **d** fuyu **e** mura **f** yama
      g mori **h** wan.
Set 3 **a** ohayou/ohayō **b** sayounara/sayōnara **c** neko
      d sensei **e** inu **f** me **g** heso **h** hito **i** rei **j** nihon.

Activity 4

a kyaa kyaa	**b** shun shun	**c** shū shū
d chū chū	**e** nyaa nyaa	**f** hyū hyū
g hyoro hyoro	**h** kyoro kyoro.	

Activity 6

a kyaku	**b** kyō	**c** gyūnyū	**d** shashin
e ja ne	**f** chōshoku	**g** chūshoku	**h** hyaku
i byōin	**j** ryokō.		

Activity 7

a mizu	**b** kagi	**c** jiten	**d** denwa
e tanpopo	**f** doki doki	**g** gabu gabu.	

Activity 8

a chotto	**b** matte	**c** yappari
d gakkō	**e** ganbatte	**f** massugu.

Activity 9

a tabemasu, tabemashita **b** nomimasu, nomimashita
c mimasu, mimashita **d** kakimasu, kakimashita
e hanashimasu, hanashimashita.

Unit 6

Introduction

a earth	**b** tree	**c** woman	**d** stone
e mouth	**f** horse	**g** sun	**h** moon.

Work it out!

a 10, b 1, c 5, d 6, e 3, f 9, g 8, h 2, i 7, j 4.

Activity 1

a 6, b 9, c 4, d 10, e 8, f 3, g 1, h 5, i 2, j 7.

Activity 2

a 4, b 2, c 5, d 3, e 1.

Activity 3

a 6, b 9, c 5, d 8, e 7, f 2, g 3, h 4, i 1.

Activity 4

a 4, b 1, c 5, d 3, e 7, f 2, g 8, h 6.

Activity 5

a 2, b 8, c 5, d 7, e 4, f 3, g 1, h 6.

Activity 6

a 11, b 5, c 13, d 14, e 1, f 7, g 8, h 9, i 12, j 6, k 3, l 4, m 15, n 17, o 2, p 10, q 16.

Activity 8

a	takai	b	yasui	c	chiisai	d	ōkii
e	sukunai	f	sukoshi	g	furui	h	atarashii
i	futoi	j	hiroi	k	shiroi.		

Test

a	1 above	2 below	3 small
	4 big	5 middle (also inside)	6 dog
	7 fat	8 a little	9 axe
	10 father	11 cow	12 stand
	13 old	14 mother	15 wide
	16 white	17 rice	18 cheap, safe
	19 thread	20 pointed	21 meat
	22 hot/bitter	23 rain	24 blue
	25 country	26 sound	27 tall, expensive
	28 island	29 school	30 black
	31 bird	32 snow	33 cloud
	34 new	35 thunder	36 electric
	37 dove	38 cloudy	39 frost.

b
1 Sunday	2 Saturday	3 Wednesday
4 Tuesday	5 start school	6 primary school
7 middle school	8 high school	9 absent from school
10 study visit	11 Japan	12 China
13 America	14 Central America	
15 mother country	16 island country	17 beef
18 chicken	19 food	20 drink
21 white rice	22 drinking water	23 train
24 new car	25 secondhand car	26 carriage
27 rickshaw	28 puppy	29 calf
30 swan	31 parents	32 child
33 adult	34 boy	35 girl
36 girl	37 shopping	38 sightseeing
39 entrance	40 exit	41 holiday.

Unit 7

Introduction

1	**a** wood	**b** forest	**c** man	**d** like
	e bright	**f** listen	**g** see	**h** write
	i say/words	**j** sell	**k** read	**l** speak
	m buy	**n** rest	**o** go out	**p** study.
2	**a** person	**b** mouth	**c** earth	**d** woman
	e child	**f** sun	**g** moon	**h** tree
	i fire	**j** rice field	**k** eye	**l** say/words
	m gold	**n** car.		

Activity 1

a 6   **b** 7   **c** 4   **d** 9   **e** 12   **f** 5   **g** 10   **h** 2   **i** 3   **j** 8   **k** 11   **l** 1.

Activity 4

a	1	hat radical	2	above
b	1	vegetation	2	above
c	1	lid	2	above
d	1	village	2	right side
e	1	enclosure	2	surround
f	1	yawn	2	right side
g	1	bamboo	2	above
h	1	fire	2	below
i	1	hole	2	above
j	1	cover	2	above
k	1	vapour	2	partial surround
l	1	heart	2	below
m	1	rain	2	above.

Activity 5

1 i c   ii d   iii e   iv b   v a.
2 i a   ii b   iii d   iv c.
3 i b   ii d   iii c   iv e   v f   vi a   vii g.

Unit 8

Introduction

a 4(4)   b 12(4)   c 14(2)   d 7(2)   e 5(6)   f 13(6)   g 2(6)
h 10(6)   i 3(6)   j 15(7)   k 11(6)   l 1(4/6)   m 9(4/6)
n 6(3)   o 8(4).

Activity 1

1 h   2 c   3 j   4 k   5 m   6 l   7 b   8 c   9 a   10 d
11 n   12 f   13 o   14 g   15 a   16 i   17 e.

Activity 2

1 e   2 f   3 j   4 o   5 n   6 l   7 i   8 a   9 h   10 g   11 k
12 d   13 m   14 b   15 c.

Activity 4

1 d, 2 b, 3 g, 4 e, 5 f, 6 h, 7 c, 8 a.

Activity 5

1 c, 2 e, 3 b, 4 a, 5 d.

Activity 6

1 toilet	2 entrance	3 toilet
4 'Thundergate'	5 push	6 pull
7 south gate	8 north gate	
9 Hiroshima, Osaka	10 grilled (food)	
11 railway station	12 Fuji Bank	
13 opening times	14 international phone	
15 unreserved	16 unoccupied taxi	
17 Japanese-style room	18 no admittance	19 no smoking.

Unit 9

Introduction

1 loanwords; foreign names; to make words stand out; plant/
animal classification.
2 part of 漢字.
3 46.

Work it out!

(in order from top) e, d, a, f, b, c.

Activity 1

skirt(e) suit(f) steak(c) cake(a) ice(d) toast(b).

Activity 2

Set 1 1 g, 2 f, 3 b, 4 c, 5 a, 6 e, 7 d.
Set 2 1 c, 2 e, 3 d, 4 b, 5 a.
Set 3 1 f, 2 g, 3 d, 4 a, 5 c, 6 b, 7 h, 8 e.

Activity 4

1 i d ii c iii a iv e v b.
2 i c ii e iii a iv d v b.
3 i f ii b iii e iv d v a vi c vii g.
4 i c ii e iii a iv d v g vi b vii f.
5 i g ii b iii i iv e v j vi a vii k viii h ix f x l
   xi c xii d.
6 i a ii c iii e iv d v f vi b.
7 i b ii e iii a iv c v d.
8 i a ii c iii e iv d v b.

Activity 6

1 h, 2 j, 3 a, 4 c, 5 i, 6 g, 7 b, 8 e, 9 f, 10 d.

Activity 7

1 i, 2 g, 3 j, 4 a, 5 e, 6 d, 7 b, 8 c, 9 f, 10 h.

Activity 8

1 g, 2 b, 3 h, 4 a, 5 l, 6 k, 7 i, 8 e, 9 c, 10 d, 11 f, 12 j.

Activity 9

1 eh 2 ai 3 ce 4 gb 5 ic 6 hj 7 dg 8 jd 9 fa 10 bf.

Activity 10

1 Luna	2 hot, iced	3 milk, lemon
4 600 yen	5 400 yen	6 cheese, ham, mixed
7 800 yen	8 350 + 600 + 700 = 1650 yen	
9 your choice	10 parfait, apple pie.	

Activity 11

1 Toyota	2 Sony	3 Casio
4 National	5 Sanyo	6 Mitsubishi.

Activity 12

1 2, 4, 6	2 3
3 printers, software	4 6
5 TV, video, laserdiscs	6 2
7 1	8 2: basement, floor 1
9 fax machines	10 basement.

Activity 13

a 2 Philippines peso,	b 4 America dollar,
c 1 England (UK) pound,	d 5 Switzerland franc,
e 6 India rupee,	f 3 Italy euro.

Activity 14

(*from top*): America dollar, euro, England pound, Swiss franc, Canada dollar, Mexico peso, Australia dollar, New Zealand dollar, South Africa rand, Saudi Arabia rial, India rupee, Thai baht, Singapore dollar, Malaysia ringgit, Indonesia rupiah, Philippine peso.

Activity 15

1 McDonald's	2 karaoke	3 opening sale
4 videos and books	5 recycle	6 a curry house
7 Valentine's Day	8 beer	9 dessert
10 E-mail	11 piano	12 Toyota
13 single malt	14 wine	15 Christmas tree
16 City of Angels, Nicholas Cage, Meg Ryan.		

Unit 10

Activity 1

1 a book b read c say.

Activity 2

1 a water	b jewel (ball)	c fire		d finger
e test	f tissue	g frying pan.		

Activity 3

1 a drink/1 b person/3 c eye/3 d enter/2 e tea/5
f convenience/mail/1 g big/1 h go out/2 i time/2.
3d 1/v, 2/vii, 3/vi, 4/iv, 5/i, 6/iii, 7/ii.
5c 1/vi, 2/iii, 3/i, 4/iv, 5/vii, 6/v, 7/ii.

Activity 4

1   a Osaka   b Tokyo   c Sapporo   d Kyoto.
3b i cloudy later sunny   ii sunny later cloudy
    iii sunny sometimes cloudy   iv rainy later cloudy.
3c i two of: Nagoya, Fukuoka, Sapporo   ii Kobe, Nara.
4a i north   ii south   iii gold/Friday   iv earth/Saturday
    v moon/Monday   vi fire/Tuesday   vii water/Wednesday.
4c All are cloudy later sunny.
4d i cloudy sometimes sunny   ii sunny sometimes cloudy
    iii cloudy sometimes rainy   iv cloudy sometimes sunny
    v sunny sometimes cloudy   vi cloudy.
4e Sunday: North Kyoto and North Shiga.
5a 28th, 21:00 or 9 o'clock.
5b i sunny/fine   ii cloudy (cloud)   iii rain   iv thunder   v snow.
6i a 29th   b cloud   c tall (high)   d fine   e weather   f above.

Activity 5

a	New Year	b	bright	c	hand	d	read
e	previous	f	Japan	g	eye	h	time
i	go	j	think	k	meet	l	enjoy
m	spirit	n	year	o	dawn	p	Yamamoto
q	child.	7	order = g, d, b, i, e, a, c, f, h.				

Activity 6

1   a   mountain   b look   c cloud   d morning   e sun
    f flower. Sample translation: Cherry blossom, cherry
    blossom, over fields and hills, I survey the endless scene
    (or: as far as the eye can see; or: an endless scene). (like) mist
    or cloud, fragrant in the morning sun, cherry blossom,
    cherry blossom, in full bloom.

Activity 7

I   1a blue/green   b rice field   c middle
     d one. Sample translation: The coolness, In the middle of a
     green rice field, one pine tree.
II   1a old   b water
     c sound. Translation: An old pond, A frog dives in, The
     sound of water.
III 1a wind   b water
     c blue. Translation: The evening breeze . . . , water laps
     against the legs of a blue heron.
IV   1a travel   b man
     c needle. Translation: An autumn night . . . , A travelling
     man's, Needlework.

A unit-by-unit summary of main 漢字 including: number of strokes (in brackets), on and kun readings, English meanings and jukugo (compound word) examples.

* For stroke order of main 漢字 refer to the writing sections of each unit. The stroke order for those 漢字 in Units 1 and 2 which don't appear in the writing sections is given in these charts (labelled 'pic').

** On readings (*onyomi*) are given in capitals, kun readings (*kunyomi*) in lower case. The bracketed part of a kun reading indicates the part written in hiragana (dictionary form is given for verbs).

Unit 1

山　SAN, **yama;**
(3)　*mountain*
川　SEN, **kawa, gawa;**
(3)　*river*
日　NICHI, JITSU, **hi, bi, ka;**
(4)　*day, sun*
月　GETSU, GATSU, **tsuki;**
(4)　*month, moon*　　　　　　[pic.1]
土　DO, TO, **tsuchi;**
(3)　*earth, ground*
竹　CHIKU, **take;**
(6)　*bamboo*　　　　　　　　[pic.2]
木　MOKU, BOKU, **ki;**
(4)　*tree, wood*
林　RIN, **hayashi, bayashi;**
(8)　*woods*

森 SHIN, mori;
(12) *forest*

水 SUI, mizu;
(4) *water*

田 DEN, ta/da;
(5) *rice field*

金 KIN, KON, kane;
(8) *gold, money* [pic.3]

火 KA, hi, bi;
(4) *fire* [pic.4]

石 SEKI, SHAKU, ishi, koku;
(5) *stone*

月 月 丿 冂 月 月
pic.1

竹 竹 丿 ⺊ ⺊ ⺮ ⺮ 竹
pic.2

金 金 丿 人 人 今 全 全 金 金
pic.3

火 火 丶 丶丶 ⺣ 火
pic.4

Unit 2

口 KŌ, KU, kuchi, guchi;
(3) *mouth*

足 SOKU (ZOKU), ashi, ta (riru);
(7) *foot (leg)* [pic.5]

目 MOKU, me;
(5) *eye*

女 JO, NYO, onna;
woman [pic.6]

子 SHI, SU, ko;
(3) *child* [pic.7]

人	NIN, JIN, hito;	
(2)	*person*	
耳	JI, mimi;	
(6)	*ear*	[pic.8]
手	SHU, te;	
(4)	*hand*	
力	RYOKU, RIKI, chikara;	
(2)	*power, strength*	[pic.9]
車	SHA, kuruma;	
(7)	*vehicle, car*	[pic.10]
馬	BA, uma;	
(10)	*horse*	[pic.11]
門	MON, kado;	
(8)	*gate*	
男	DAN, NAN, otoko;	
(7)	*man*	[pic.12]
好	KŌ, kono(mu);	
(6)	*like, love*	[pic.13]
明	MEI, MYŌ, aka(rui), aki(raka);	
(8)	*bright, light*	[pic.14]
本	HON, moto;	
(5)	*root, origin, main, book*	[pic.15]

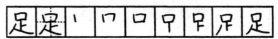

pic.5

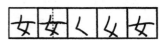

pic.6

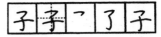

pic.7

pic.8

力 力 つ 力

pic.9

pic.10

pic.11

pic.12

pic.13

pic.14

pic.15

Unit 3

一 ICHI, **hito(tsu)**;
(1) *one*
二 NI, **futa(tsu)**;
(2) *two*
三 SAN, **mit(tsu)**;
(3) *three*
四 SHI, **yon, yo, yot(tsu)**;
(5) *four*
五 GO, **itsu(tsu)**;
(4) *five*
六 ROKU, **mut(tsu)**;
(4) *six*
七 SHICHI, **nana(tsu)**;
(2) *seven*

八   HACHI, yat(tsu);
(2)   *eight*
九   KYŪ, KU; kokono (tsu);
(2)   *nine*
十   JŪ, tō;
(2)   *ten*
百   HYAKU;
(6)   *hundred*
千   SEN, chi;
(3)   *thousand*
万   MAN, BAN;
(3)   *ten thousand, all*
円   EN;
(4)   *yen, circle*
年   NEN, toshi;
(6)   *year, age*

Unit 4

聞   BUN, ki(ku);
(14)   *hear, listen*
見   KEN, mi(ru);
(7)   *look, see, watch*
書   SHO, ka(ku);
(10)   *write*
言   GEN, (GON), i(u), koto;
(7)   *say*
学   GAKU, mana(bu);
(8)   *study, learn*
買   BAI, ka(u);
(12)   *buy*
休   KYŪ, yasu(mu);
(6)   *rest*
出   SHUTSU, de(ru), da(su);
(5)   *go / come out*
売   BAI, u(ru);
(7)   *sell*
読   DOKU, yo(mu);
(14)   *read*
話   WA, hanashi, hana(su);
(13)   *talk*
食   SHOKU, ta(beru);
(9)   *eat*

飲 IN, no(mu);
(12) *drink*
入 NYŪ, i(ru), hai(ru);
(2) *enter, put in*
物 BUTSU, MOTSU, mono;
(8) *thing*

Unit 6

立 RITSU, ta(tsu), tachi;
(5) *stand (up)*
高 KŌ, taka(i);
(10) *high, expensive*
鳥 CHŌ, tori;
(11) *bird*
米 BEI, MAI, kome;
(6) *rice*
大 DAI, TAI, ō(kii);
(3) *big, great*
斤 KIN, ono;
(4) *axe*
牛 GYŪ, ushi;
(4) *cow, cattle*
古 KO, furu(i);
(5) *old*
糸 SHI, ito;
(6) *thread*
小 SHŌ, chii(sai), ko, o;
(3) *small*
母 BO, haha, (o)kā(san);
(5) *mother*
安 AN, yasu(i);
(6) *cheap, safe*
広 KŌ, hiro(i);
(5) *wide, spacious*
新 SHIN, atara(shii);
(13) *new*
黒 KOKU, kuro(i);
(11) *black*
白 HAKU, BYAKU, shiro(i), jiro;
(5) *white*

青 SEI, SHŌ, ao(i);
(8) *blue, green, inexperienced*
父 FU, chichi, tō, (o)tō(san);
(4) *father*
雨 U, ame;
(8) *rain*
上 JŌ, ue, nobo (ru), a(garu);
(3) *above, on, top*
下 KA, GE, shita, moto, kuda(ru);
(3) *below, under, go down*
中 CHŪ, naka;
(4) *inside, middle, within*
雲 UN, kumo;
(12) *cloud;*
曇 DON, kumo(ri);
(16) *cloudy weather*
雷 RAI, kaminari;
(13) *thunder*
雪 SETSU, yuki;
(11) *snow*
電 DEN;
(13) *electric*
犬 KEN, inu;
(4) *dog*
島 TŌ, shima, jima;
(10) *island*
音 ON, IN, oto, ne;
(9) *sound*
辛 SHIN, kara(i);
(7) *hot, bitter, spicy;*
霜 SŌ, shimo;
(17) *frost*
少 SHŌ, suku(nai), suko(shi);
(4) *few, a little*
太 TAI, TA, futo(i);
(4) *fat, deep (voice)*
国 KOKU, kuni, guni;
(8) *country*
肉 NIKU;
(6) *meat, flesh*
校 KŌ;
(10) *school*

Unit 7

信 SHIN, shin(jiru);
(9) *believe, trust;*

唱 SHŌ, tona(eru);
(11) *chant, recite;*

畑 hata, hatake;
(9) *cultivated field*

談 DAN;
(15) *talk, discussion*

孫 SON, mago;
(10) *grandchild*

鳴 MEI, na(ku);
(14) *cry, chirp*

炎 EN, honō;
(8) *blaze, flame*

焚 FUN, ta(ku), ya(ku);
(12) *burn, kindle*

語 GO; kata(ru);
(14) *language, word, tell*

埋 MAI, u(meru);
(10) *bury / be buried*

旦 TAN;
(5) *dawn*

姦 KAN;
(9) *wicked, noisy*

活 KATSU;
(9) *live, energy*

体 TAI, TEI, karada;
(7) *body*

町 CHŌ, machi;
(7) *town*

村 SON, mura;
(7) *village*

妹 MAI, imōto;
(8) *younger sister*

灯 TŌ, hi;
(6) *lamp, light*

折 SETSU, o(ru);
(7) *fold, snap, bend*

眠 MIN, nemu(i);
(10) *sleep(y)*

吠 HAI, ho(eru);
(7) *bark*

肘　CHŌ, hiji
(7)　*elbow*
泊　HAKU, to(maru);
(8)　*stay at, put up*
針　SHIN, hari;
(10)　*needle*
転　TEN, koro(garu);
(11)　*turn, change*
時　JI, toki, doki;
(10)　*time*

Unit 8

店　TEN, mise;
(8)　*shop, store*
屋　OKU, ya;
(9)　*shop*
局　KYOKU;
(7)　*bureau, office*
所　SHO, JO, tokoro;
(8)　*place*
場　JŌ, ba;
(12)　*place*
館　KAN;
(16)　*hall, large building*
園　EN, sono;
(13)　*garden*
市　SHI, ichi;
(5)　*city, market*
工　KŌ, KU;
(3)　*construction*
公　KŌ, ōyake;
(4)　*public*
図　TO, ZU, haka(ru);
(7)　*drawing, map*
魚　GYO, sakana, uo;
(11)　*fish*
酒　SHU, sake, saka;
(10)　*rice wine, alcohol*
茶　CHA;
(9)　*tea*
薬　YAKU, kusuri;
(16)　*medicine*

洗 SEN, ara(u);
(9) *wash*

主 SHU, nushi;
(5) *master, owner*

駐 CHŪ;
(15) *reside, stop-over*

住 JŪ, su(mu);
(7) *reside, live*

駅 EKI;
(14) *station*

便 BEN, BIN;
(9) *convenience, mail*

行 KŌ, GYŌ, AN, i(ku), yu(ku), okona(u);
(6) *go, hold*

室 SHITSU;
(9) *room*

内 NAI, DAI, uchi;
(4) *inside, home*

外 GAI, GE, soto, hoka;
(5) *outside, foreign*

席 SEKI;
(10) *seat, place*

料 RYŌ;
(10) *charge, materials*

北 HOKU, BOKU, kita;
(5) *north*

南 NAN, minami;
(9) *south*

東 TŌ, higashi;
(8) *east*

西 SEI, SAI, nishi;
(6) *west*

禁 KIN;
(13) *forbidden*

右 U, YŪ, migi;
(5) *right*

左 SA, hidari;
(5) *left*

開 KAI, a (keru), hira, (ku);
(12) *open*

閉 HEI, shi (meru), to (jiru);
(11) *close*

The number in brackets indicates the page where the word first appears.

D

dawn (90)   day (2)   dealer (52)   decree (95)   departure (118)   discussion (90)   dog (79)   domestic (112)   dormant volcano (52)   dove (79)   down (105)   drawing (107)   drink (49)   drinking place (107)   drinking water (52)   drinks (51)   drought (95)   dry weather (95)   dwell (108)

E

ear (14)   earth (3)   east (115)   eat (48)   eating and drinking (52)   eight (30)   elbow (92)   electric (79)   elementary school (82)   emotion (95)   enter (49)   entrance (52)   entrance fee (114)   exit (52)   explosion (96)   express (118)   eye (14)

F

factory (107)   fare adjustment office (110)   fat (80)   father (77)   fee (111)   feeling (95)   few (79)   fine weather (95)   fire (4)   fish (107)   fishmonger (107)   five (30)   flame (89)   flesh (82)   fold (92)   food (48, 51)   foot (14)   forbidden (117)   foreign (112)   foreign exchange (112)   forest (4)   four (30)   Friday (6)   frost (79)

G

garden (105)   gate (14)   gateway (16)   girl (16, 81)   go (108)   go in (49)   going in and out (52)   gold (5)   good at (81)   go out (45)   grandchild (90)   greengrocer (107)   grilled (118)   ground (4)

H

hall (105)   hand (14)   hear (45)   heavy rain (80)   high (75)   high school (82)   history (90)   hold (94)   holiday (45, 52)   horse (14)   horse power (16)   hot (79)   hour (92)   hundred (34)

I

imperial edict (95)   information (109)   inherit (95)   inn, Japanese (110)   inside (78)   international phone (112)   invite (95)   island (79)   island country (81)   items for sale (51)

J

Japan (16)   Japanese: bath (114), cuisine (115), inn (111), person (16), room (112), style (115)   junior high school (82)

K

kindle (90)   kiosk (107)

L

lamp (92)   language (90)   large building (105)   left (118) left luggage (113)   lesson (90)   library (107)   like (15)   listen (45)   liquor store (107)   live (92)   liver (96)   long-distance train (111)   look (45)   love (15)   luggage (113)

M

make (96)   mail (108)   man (15)   manpower (16)   map (107) market (107, 108)   marsh (95)   master (108)   meat (82) medicine (107)   middle (78)   middle school (82)   mischief (96)   Monday (5)   money (4)   money exchange (109) month (2)   mother (76)   mother country (81)   mountain (4) moon (2)   mouth (14)   museum (110)

N

narrative (90)   needle (92)   new (77)   new car (81) newspaper (81)   new year (81)   nine (30)   noise (79)   north (116)   not allowed (117)

O

occupied taxi (111)   office (105)   old (75)   older (81)   one (30)   on top (78)   open (118)   open for business (118) origin (15)

P

paddy field (16)   pair (52)   pale (80)   parcel (113)   parents (80)   park (107)   passport control (112)   person (14) perspire (96)   pharmacy (107)   pigeon (79)   place (105) poem (90)   pointed (79)   pole (96)   polished rice (80) population (16)   post office (109)   powder room (114)

W

wait (115)   waiting room (115)   wash (107)   watch (45)
water (3)   water power (16)   Wednesday (6)   west (116)
western-style (115) + cuisine (115), room (112)   white (77)
white rice (80, 95)   wickedness (90, 96)   wide (76)   wine
(107)   wine shop (107)   woman (14)   wood/s (3)   words
(45)   write (48)   writing (51)

Y

yen (34)   year (36)   yesterday (96)   younger sister (92)
youth (81)

taking it further

There is a wealth of workbooks, internet sites and software packages that can help you to take your study of Japanese script further. The suggestions below are taken from my own teaching experience and feedback from students and other teachers. It is by no means an exhaustive list and the internet in particular is continuously producing new and often improved possibilities. However, the list does include some of the real 'backbones' and classics for learning to read and write Japanese.

Books

1 Spoken language

Try other titles in Hodder and Stoughton's **teach yourself series**:

- *Teach Yourself Beginner's Japanese*, Helen Gilhooly, 2002. This includes a chapter on script.
- *Teach Yourself Instant Japanese*, Elisabeth Smith, 1998.
- *Teach Yourself Japanese*, Helen Ballhatchet and Stefan Kaiser, 2001.

2 Written language – kana scripts

There are various good kana workbooks which take you systematically through the learning process, including the following:

- *Easy Hiragana*, Fujihiko Kaneda et al., McGraw-Hill, 1989
- *Easy Katakana*, Tina Wells et al., McGraw-Hill, 1989
- *Let's Learn Hiragana, Let's Learn Katakana* (2 volumes), YK Mitamura, Kodansha Europe, 1992.

- *Hiragana Gambatte, Katakana Gambatte* (2 volumes), Deleece Batt, Kodansha Europe, 1994. Teaches through manga-style art and mini-articles on Japanese society and culture.
- *Hiragana/Katakana in 48 minutes* (2 volumes), Hiroko C Quackenbush et al, Curriculum Corporation, 1989. Set of flashcards for memorizing kana through picture and sound association.
- *Introduction to Written Japanese* (2 volumes), Jim Gleeson, Tuttle Language Library, 1997.
- *Kana Can Be Easy*, Kunihiko Ogawa, The Japan Times, 1992. Teaches kana through mnemonics and picture stories.
- *All About Katakana*, Anne M Stewart, Kodansha Europe, 1993. How to memorize katakana quickly with over 1000 examples of its usage.

3 Written language – kanji

- *250 Essential Kanji for Everyday Use*, Tuttle & Co., 1998. Includes many illustrations and photos of everyday kanji such as signs and maps, as well as stroke order, readings and compounds of 250 common kanji.
- *Basic Kanji Book 500* (2 volumes), Chieko Kano et al, Bonjinsha. A workbook which introduces 12–15 themed kanji per chapter with background stories and exercises to help consolidate learning.
- *Essential Kanji*, P G O'Neil, Weatherhill, 1974. A systematic reference book of the 2000 essential kanji.
- *A Guide to Remembering the Japanese Characters*, Kenneth G Henshall, Tuttle & Co., 1998. Another systematic reference which also includes mnemonics and stories to explain the development of each kanji and help you to remember them.
- *Remembering the Kanji*, James W Heisig, Japan Publications Trading Company, 1990. This course teaches you how to remember kanji through imaginative and memorable pictures and stories.
- *Let's Learn Kanji*, JY and YK Mitamura, 1997. A new approach to learning 250 basic kanji through radicals and components.
- *Japan in Your Pocket – Illustrated Japanese Characters*, Japan Travel Bureau, Inc, 1993. A pocket-sized book which introduces everyday kanji via their radicals in an easy-to-read format.

- *Read Japanese Today*, Len Walsh, Tuttle & Co., 1969. Another pocket-sized book which introduces kanji through pictures and mnemonics.

4 Texts and readers (for intermediate and advanced learners)

- *Kanji from the Start, a Comprehensive Japanese Reader*, Martin Lam and Shimizu Kaoru, Kodansha International, 1995. This introduces new kanji in each chapter along with text incorporating them plus grammar explanations.
- *An Introduction to Newspaper Japanese*, O and N Mizutami, Japan Times, 1986. Helps the intermediate learner decipher newspaper headings and articles.
- *Tottochan*, Kuroyanagi Tetsuko, Kodansha. The best-selling novel of the author's school life in 1950s Japan which is available in Japanese, English and bilingual versions.
- *Dondon Yomeru*, Iroirona Hanashi, Akimoto Miharu, 1991. This is a compilation of simplified short stories by famous Japanese novelists.

The Kodansha *Power Japanese* series has a number of Japanese readers including:

- *Kanji Idioms*, George Wallace and Kayoko Kimiya, 1995 – introduces lots of four-character compound words with explanations and translations of their use.
- *Read Real Japanese*, Janet Ashby, 1994 – a series of short essays with English translations and grammar explanations from famous Japanese personalities such as the musician, Sakamoto Ryuichi and the female novelist, Yoshimoto Banana.

5 Magazines (available from Japanese bookshops)

- *Hiragana Times* (monthly). Written in kana, kanji and English and aimed at cross-cultural communication. Has its own website: **www.hiraganatimes.com/**.
- *The Nihongo Journal* (monthly, available with cassette. Website: **www.alc.co.jp/nj/**). Language instruction for learners of all levels with up-to-date information about Japan.
- *Mangajin* (quarterly). Extracts from popular Japanese comics with translation, grammar and cultural explanations in English.

6 Dictionaries

- *The Oxford Starter Japanese Dictionary*, Jonathan Bunt, Oxford University Press, 2000. Two-way dictionary especially written for students of Japanese, with examples of how the words are used in practice. Entries in script and English.
- *Webster's New World Compact Japanese Dictionary*, 1997. Two-way dictionary, entries in *romaji*, script and English.
- *Pictorial Japanese and English Dictionary*, ed. John Pheby, Oxford University Press, 1997.
- *Dictionary of Basic Japanese Grammar*, S Makino and M Tsutsui, The Japan Times, 1992.
- *Kodansha Kanji Learner's Dictionary*, Jack Halpern, Kodansha International, 2002.
- *The New Nelson Japanese–English Character Dictionary*, Andrew N Nelson, Tuttle & Co, 1997. An update of the classic kanji dictionary with contemporary definitions.
- *The Compact Nelson, Japanese–English Character Dictionary*, John H Haig, Tuttle & Co. A portable version of Nelson's classic kanji dictionary.
- *The Kanji Dictionary*, Mark Spahn & Wolfgang Hadamitzky, Tuttle & Co, 1996. 47,000+ kanji compounds.
- *Canon Wordtank Super Electronic Dictionary*. Electronic dictionaries are very popular in Japan but mainly are created for Japanese native speakers. The *Canon Wordtank* is for foreign learners of Japanese and features include two-way dictionaries, kanji dictionary and useful expressions.

7 General

- *Teach Yourself Japanese Language, Life & Culture*, Helen Gilhooly, Hodder and Stoughton, 2002. For a general introduction to all aspects of Japanese life and society.
- *Kodansha Bilingual Encyclopedia of Japan*, 1998. An easy-to-read comprehensive encyclopedia with entries and index in English and Japanese.
- *Kodansha Encyclopedia of Japan*, 1999. A detailed and comprehensive English language reference book on all aspects of Japan. Also available on CD-ROM with various extras such as dictionary and links to worldwide web.
- *Japan Made Easy – All You Need to Know to Enjoy Japan*, Boye Lafayette De Mente, Passport Books, 1995. Practical advice and information for visiting Japan including lots of 'dos and don'ts'.

- *Japan*, Chris Taylor, Lonely Planet, 1997. Traveller's guidebook includes lots of interesting facts and advice about Japan.

Websites

The internet is constantly changing and developing and it is always worth doing searches for new Japanese language sites but some good current ones include:

- *Japanese Writing Tutor Site*: **members.aol.com/writejapan/**. This is an excellent site for learning how to write hiragana and katakana (a 'virtual' calligraphy brush demonstrates the shape and stroke order of each symbol for you to copy) and also includes an introduction to 45 basic kanji.
- *Jim Breen's Japanese Page*: **www.csse.monash.edu.au/~jwb/japanese.html** (or do a search for Jim Breen). This site includes instructions on how to download a freeware Japanese word processing programme (JWPce), a Japanese–English dictionary and links to many other Japanese learning sites and free/share ware.
- Web Resources for Teaching and Learning of Japanese Language (compiled by Anai Sensei, Essex University): **www.essex.ac.uk/centres/japan/resources/menu.html**.
- A useful kanji tutor site: **www.kanjicards.com**.
- *Write hiragana*: **www.jfet.org.uk/FS1.html**.
- JIN (Japan Information Network): **www.jinjapan.org/index.html**. Various information about Japan with links to Japanese language sites found under *Japan Web Navigator – Education*.
- For information on the Japanese Language Proficiency Tests (there are four levels from beginners to advanced): **www.soas.ac.uk/centres/Japan/proficiency.html**.

Software

- *Kanakun*, Fujitsu, Aus 1998, CD-ROM. Hiragana and Katakana tutor which has animated stroke order, pronunciation practice and lots of recognition games.
- *Kantaro*, Macquarie University, Sydney, Fujitsu 1993, CD-ROM × 3. Interactive kanji learning programme which

teaches kanji through picture association and includes writing practice, readings and compounds.

- *Kanji Sensei 3.0*, Frank Potter, 1996, Pacific Rim Systems, 2 × floppy disks. This is becoming more difficult to get hold of but it worth persisting because it is an excellent kanji tutor which works systematically and thematically through basic kanji, giving stroke order demonstrations and practice and opportunities to test yourself against the computer tutor.
- *Free Light Japanese*, Chilly Mazarin, Free Light software, 1995, CD-ROM. A Japanese learning programme for Windows which teaches hiragana, katakana and kanji with drills and pictures.
- *Blackbelt Japanese*, Rising Wave Inc., Honolulu 1995, CD-ROM. Language-learning games for recognition (but not writing practice) of the Japanese writing system.
- *Talk Now! Learn Japanese*, Eurotalk Interactive, London 1998, CD-ROM. Beginners' conversational Japanese but adapted from European languages and so not culturally specific.

There are also a number of Japanese word-processing packages available which either work independently of Windows or are Windows compatible. They can also be used for sending e-mail in Japanese listed (providing the receiver has compatible software). The ones below also have other features such as dictionaries and kanji look-up facilities:

- *NJStar*, NJStar Software Corp., 1991–99. Information (including downloadable trial program) available at their website at **www.njstar.com**. This package works separately to Windows but it is possible to cut and paste into Windows and it has a range of advanced features such as various fonts and dictionaries.
- *Kanji Kit 2000*, Japanese Utility for English Windows, Pacific Software Publishing, Inc.: **www.pspinc.com/lsg**. Works with many Windows applications such as Photoshop, Corel Draw, Internet Explorer, MS Excel/Word etc. Can be used to create Japanese sites and customized kanji characters.
- *JWPce* (see website section above for contact details). A basic word-processing package for typing in Japanese script (works separately to Windows) but with useful features such as dictionaries and kanji search facility.

Organizations

- Japanese embassies across the world have JICC (Japan Information and Cultural Centres) from which you can borrow books and videos as well as subscribe to a number of magazines and newsletters and find out about Japanese classes, societies and other organizations in your country. Go to **www.embjapan.org** and you will find links to every JICC and Japanese embassy in the world.
- Japan National Tourist Organization (JNTO): **www.jnto.go.jp/**
- For information on the JET programme (teaching English in Japan): **www.jetprogramme.org/**

beginner's japanese
helen gilhooly

- Are you new to language learning?
- Do you want lots of practice and examples?
- Do you want to improve your confidence to speak?

Beginner's Japanese is written for the complete beginner who wants to move at a steady pace and have lots of opportunity to practise. The grammar is explained clearly and does not assume that you have studied a language before. You will learn everything you need to get the most out of a holiday or to go on to further study.

teach yourself

world cultures: japan
helen gilhooly

- Are you interested in the story of Japan and the Japanese?
- Do you want to understand how the country works today?
- Are you planning a visit to Japan or learn Japanese?

World Cultures: Japan will give you a basic overview of Japan – the country, its language, its people and its culture – and will enrich any visit or course of study. Vocabulary lists and 'Taking it Further' sections at the end of every unit will equip you to talk and write confidently about all aspects of Japanese life.